William Penn

Three Treatises,

in which the fundamental principle, doctrines, worship, ministry and discipline of the people called Quakers, are plainly declared

William Penn

Three Treatises,
in which the fundamental principle, doctrines, worship, ministry and discipline of the people called Quakers, are plainly declared

ISBN/EAN: 9783337411206

Printed in Europe, USA, Canada, Australia, Japan

Cover: Foto ©Lupo / pixelio.de

More available books at **www.hansebooks.com**

TREATISE

IN WHICH

The FUNDAMENTAL PRINCIPLE, DOCTRINES, WORSHIP, MINISTRY and DISCIPLINE of the People called

QUAKERS,

ARE PLAINLY DECLARED.

The FIRST,
By WILLIAM PENN, in *England*;

The SECOND,
By ROBERT BARCLAY, in *Scotland*;

The THIRD,
By JOSEPH PIKE, in *Ireland*.

WILMINGTON,
Re-printed by JAMES ADAMS.
M,DCC,LXXXIII.

A BRIEF ACCOUNT

OF THE

RISE and PROGRESS

Of the PEOPLE called

QUAKERS,

IN WHICH

Their *Fundamental Principle, Doctrines, Worship, Ministry* and *Discipline,* are plainly declared.

With a Summary RELATION

Of the Former Dispensations of GOD in the World, by Way of *Introduction.*

As unknown, and yet well known. 2 Cor. vi. 9.

The Seventh Edition.

By WILLIAM PENN.

WILMINGTON,
Re-printed by JAMES ADAMS,
M,DCC,LXXXIII.

AN EPISTLE TO THE READER.

READER, this following *Account* of the People called *Quakers*, &c. was wrote in the Fear and Love of God: *First*, As a standing Testimony to that ever blessed Truth, in the inward Parts, with which God, in my youthful Time, visited my Soul, and for the Sense and Love of which I was made willing, in no ordinary Way, to relinquish the Honours and Interests of the World. *Secondly*, As a Testimony for that despised People, that God has in His great Mercy gathered and united by His own blessed Spirit in the holy Profession of it; whose Fellowship I value above all Worldly Greatness. *Thirdly*, In Love and Honour to the Memory of that worthy Servant of God, *George Fox*, the first Instrument thereof, and therefore stiled by me *The great and blessed Apostle of our Day*. As this gave Birth to what is here presented to thy View, in the first Edition of it, by way of *Preface* to *George Fox*'s excellent Journal; so the Consideration of the present Usefulness of the following *Account* of the People called *Quakers*, (by Reason of the unjust Reflections of some Adversaries

An Epistle *to the* Reader.

versaries that once walked under the Profession of *Friends*) and the Exhortations that conclude it, prevailed with me to consent that it should be republished in a smaller Volume; knowing also full well that great Books, especially in these Days, grow burthensome, both to the Pockets and Minds of too many; and that there are not a few that desire (so it be at an easy Rate) to be informed about this People, that have been so much every where spoken against: But blessed be the God and Father of our Lord Jesus Christ, it is upon no worse Grounds than it was said of old Time, of the primitive *Christians*; as I hope will appear to every sober and considerate Reader. Our Business, after all the ill Usage we have met with, being the Realities of Religion, an effectual Change before our last and great Change: That all may come to an inward sensible and experimental Knowledge of God, through the Convictions and Operations of the Light and Spirit of Christ in themselves; the sufficient and blessed Means given to all, that thereby all may come savingly to know the only true God, and Jesus Christ whom He hath sent, to enlighten, and redeem the World: Which Knowledge is indeed *eternal Life*——And that thou, *Reader*, may'st obtain it, is the earnest Desire of him that is ever

Thine in so good a Work,

WILLIAM PENN.

CONTENTS.

CHAP. I.

Containing a brief Account of divers Dispensations of God in the World, till the Time He was pleased to raise this despised People called Quakers.   1.

CHAP. II.

Of the Rise of this People, their fundamental Principle and Doctrine, and Practice, in twelve Points resulting from it; their Progress and Sufferings: An Expostulation with England thereupon.   14.

CHAP. III.

Of the Qualifications of their Ministry. Eleven Marks that it is Christian.   37.

CHAP. IV.

Of the Discipline and Practice of this People, as a Religious Society. The Church Power they own

The Contents.

own and exercise, and that which they reject and condemn: With the Method of their Proceedings against erring and disorderly Persons. 44.

CHAP. V.

Of the first Instrument *or* Person *by whom* God *was pleased to gather this* People *into the Way they profess. His Name* George Fox; *his many excellent Qualifications; shewing a divine, and not an human Power to have been their Original in him. His Troubles and Sufferings both from without and within. His* End *and* Triumph. 51.

CHAP. VI.

Containing five *several* Exhortations. *First,* General, *reminding this People of their primitive Integrity and Simplicity. Secondly, in* Particular, *To the* Ministry. *Thirdly, To the* Young Convinced.— *Fourthly, To the* Children *of* Friends. *Fifthly, To those that are yet* Strangers *to this* People *and* Way; *to whom this Book (and that it was.* Preface *to in its first Edition) may come. All the several Exhortations accommodated to their several States and Conditions; that all may answer the End of God's Glory and their own Salvation.* 66.

A

A Brief ACCOUNT, &c.

CHAP. I.

Containing a brief Account of divers Dispensations of GOD *in the World, to the Time He was pleased to raise this despised People, called* QUAKERS.

DIVERS have been the Dispensations of God since the Creation of the World unto the Sons of Men; but the great End of all of them has been the *Renown of His own excellent Name in the Creation and Restoration of Man*: Man, the Emblem of Himself, as a God on Earth, and the Glory of all His Works. The World began with Innocency: All was then good that the good God had made: And as He blessed the Works of His Hands, so their Natures and Harmony magnified Him their Creator. Then the Morning Stars sang together for Joy, and all Parts of His Works said *Amen* to His Law. Not a Jarr in the whole Frame; but Man in Paradise, the Beasts in the Field, the Fowl in the Air, the Fish in the Sea, the Lights in the Heavens, the Fruits of the Earth; yea, the Air, the Earth, the Water and Fire worshipped, praised and exalted His *Power, Wisdom* and *Goodness*. O holy Sabbath, O holy Day to the Lord!

But this happy State lasted not long: For Man,

the Crown and Glory of the Whole, being tempted to aspire above his Place, unhappily yielded against Command and Duty, as well as Interest and Felicity, and so fell below it; lost the divine Image, the Wisdom, Power and Purity he was made in. By which, being no longer fit for Paradise, he was expelled that Garden of God, his proper Dwelling and Residence, and was driven out, as a poor Vagabond, from the Presence of the Lord, to wander in the Earth, the Habitation of Beasts.

Yet God that made him had Pity on him; for He seeing Man was deceived, and that it was not of Malice, or an *original Presumption* in him, but through the Subtilty of the Serpent (who had first fallen from his own State, and by the Mediation of the Woman, Man's own Nature and Companion, whom the Serpent had first deluded) in His infinite Goodness and Wisdom provided a Way to repair the Breach, recover the Loss, and restore fallen Man again by a *nobler and more excellent* Adam, promised to be born of a Woman; that as by Means of a Woman the evil One had prevailed upon Man, by a Woman also He should come into the World, who would prevail against him and *bruise his Head*, and deliver Man from his Power: And which, in a signal Manner, by the Dispensation of the Son of God in the Flesh, in the Fulness of Time, was personally and fully accomplished by Him, and in Him, as Man's Saviour and Redeemer.

But His Power was not limited, in the Manifestation of it, to that Time; for both before and since His blessed Manifestation in the Flesh, He has been

been the *Light* and *Life*, the *Rock* and *Strength*, of all that ever feared God: Was present with them in their Temptations, followed them in their Travels and Afflictions, and supported and carried them through and over the Difficulties that have attended them in their earthly Pilgrimage. By this *Abel*'s Heart excelled *Cain*'s, and *Seth* obtained the Pre-eminence, and *Enoch* walked with God. It was this that strove with the old World, and which they rebelled against, and which sanctified and instructed *Noah* to Salvation.

But the outward Dispensation that followed the benighted State of Man, after his Fall, especially among the *Patriarchs*, was generally that of *Angels*; as the Scriptures of the Old Testament do in many Places express, as to *Abraham*, *Jacob*, &c. The next was that of the *Law* by *Moses*, which was also delivered by Angels, as the Apostle tells us. This Dispensation was much outward, and suited to a low and servile State; called therefore by the Apostle *Paul*, that of a *School-master*, which was to point out and prepare that People to look and long for the MESSIAH, who would deliver them from the Servitude of a ceremonious and imperfect Dispensation, by knowing the Realities of those mysterious Representations in themselves. In this Time the Law was written on Stone, the Temple built with Hands, attended with an outward *Priesthood* and *external* Rites and Ceremonies, that were *Shadows of the good Things that were to come*, and were only to serve till the Seed came, or the more excellent and general Manifestation of Christ, to whom was the Promise, and to all Men only in Him, in whom it was

was *Yea* and *Amen*, even *Life* from *Death*, *Immortality* and *Eternal Life*.

This the *Prophets* foresaw, and comforted the believing *Jews* in the Certainty of it; which was the Top of the *Mosaical* Dispensation, which ended in *John's* Ministry, the Fore-runner of the Messiah, as *John's* was finished in Him, the Fulness of all. And then God, that at sundry Times, and in divers Manners had spoken to the Fathers by His Servants the Prophets, spoke to Men by His Son Christ Jesus, *who is Heir of all Things*; being the Gospel-Day, which is the Dispensation of *Son-ship*; bringing in thereby a nearer Testament, and a better Hope; even the Beginning of the Glory of the latter Days, and of the Restitution of all Things; yea, the *Restoration of the Kingdom unto* Israel.

Now the Spirit, that was more sparingly communicated in former Dispensations, began to be *poured forth upon all Flesh*, according to the Prophet *Joel*; and the *Light that shined in Darkness*, or but dimly before, the most gracious God caused to *shine out of Darkness* and the Day-star began to arise in the Hearts of Believers, giving unto them the Knowledge of God in the Face (or Appearance) of His Son Christ Jesus.

Now the *Poor in Spirit*, the *Meek*, the true *Mourners*, the *Hungry* and *Thirsty* after *Righteousness*, the *Peace-makers*, the *Pure in Heart*, the *Merciful* and *Persecuted*, came more especially in Remembrance before the Lord, and were sought out and blessed by him, *Israel's true Shepherd*. Old *Jerusalem* with her Children grew out of Date, and the *New Jerusalem* into Request, the Mother of the Sons of the
Gospel-

Gospel-Day. Wherefore no more at *Old Jerusalem*, nor at the *Mountain* of *Samaria*, will God be worshipped above other Places; for, behold, He is, by His own Son, declared and preached a Spirit, and that He will be known as such, and worshipped in the Spirit and in the Truth! He will now come nearer than of old Time, *and he will write His Law in the Heart, and put His Fear and Spirit in the inward Parts*, according to His Promise. Then *Signs*, *Types* and *Shadows* flew away, the Day having discovered their Insufficiency in not reaching to the *Inside of the Cup, to the cleansing of the Conscience*; and all Elementary Services were expired in and by Him that is the Substance of all.

And to this great and blessed End of the Dispensation of the Son of God, did the Apostles testify, whom He had chosen and anointed by His Spirit, to turn the *Jews* from their Prejudice and Superstition, and the *Gentiles* from their Vanity and Idolatry, to Christ's *Light* and *Spirit* that shined in them; that they might be quickned from the Sins and Trespasses in which they were dead, to serve the living God, in the *Newness* of the Spirit of Life, and walk as Children of the *Light*, and of the Day, even the Day of *Holiness*: For such *put on* Christ, the Light of the World, *and make no more Provision for the Flesh, to fulfil the Lusts thereof*. So that the *Light*, *Spirit* and *Grace*, that come by Christ, and appear in Man, were that *divine Principle*, the Apostles ministred from; and turned People's Minds unto, and in which they gathered and built up the Churches of Christ in their Day. For which Cause they advise them *not to quench the Spirit*, but to *wait for the Spirit*,

and

and *speak by the Spirit*, and *pray by the Spirit*, and *walk in the Spirit* too, as that which approved them, the truly begotten Children of God; *born not of Flesh and Blood, or of the Will of Man, but of the Will of God*; by doing His Will, and denying their own; by drinking of Christ's Cup, and being baptized with *His Baptism* of Self-denial; the Way and Path that all the Heirs of Life have ever trod to Blessedness. But alas! even in the Apostles Days, those bright Stars of the first Magnitude of the Gospel Light, some Clouds foretelling an Eclipse of this primitive Glory, began to appear, and several of them gave early Caution of it to the *Christians* of their Time, that even then there was, and yet would be more and more, a falling away from the Power of Godliness, and the Purity of that spiritual Dispensation, by such as sought to make a *fair Shew in the Flesh*, with whom the Offence of the Cross ceased. Yet with this comfortable Conclusion, that they saw beyond it a more glorious Time than ever to the true Church. Their Sight was true, and what they foretold to the Churches, gathered by them in the Name and Power of Jesus, came to pass: For *Christians* degenerated apace into *Outsides*, as *Days* and *Meats*, and divers other Ceremonies. And which was worse, they fell into *Strife* and *Contention* about them; *separating* one from another, then *envying*, and, as they had Power, *persecuting* one another to the Shame and Scandal of their common *Christianity*, and grievous Stumbling and Offence of the *Heathen*; among whom the Lord had so long and so marvellously preserved them. And having got at last the Worldly Power into their Hands, by Kings and Emperors embracing the *Christian* Profeſſion, they changed, what they could, the Kingdom of Chriſt, *which is not of this World*, into a Worldly Kingdom; or at leaſt ſtiled the Worldly Kingdom, that was in their Hands, the *Kingdom of* Chriſt, and ſo they became *Worldly*, and not true *Chriſtians*. Then *human Inventions* and *Novelties*, both in Doctrine and Worſhip, crouded faſt into the Church; a Door opened thereunto, by the Groſsneſs and Carnality that appeared then among the Generality of *Chriſtians*, who had long ſince left the Guidance of God's meek and Heavenly Spirit, *and given themſelves up to Superſtition, Will Worſhip, and voluntary Humility*. And as Superſtition is blind, ſo it is heady and furious, for all muſt ſtoop to its blind and boundleſs Zeal or periſh by it: *In the Name of the Spirit*, perſecuting the very Appearance of the Spirit of God in others, and oppoſing that in others, which they reſiſted in themſelves, *viz. The Light, Grace and Spirit of the* Lord Jeſus Chriſt; but always under the Notion of *Innovation, Hereſy, Schiſm*, or ſome ſuch *plauſible Name*. Though *Chriſtianity* allows of no Name, or Pretence whatever, for perſecuting of any Man for Matters of mere Religion, being in its very Nature, *meek, gentle* and *forbearing*; and conſiſts of *Faith, Hope* and *Charity*, which no Perſecutor can have, whilſt he remains a Perſecutor; in that a Man cannot believe well, or hope well, or have a charitable or tender Regard to another, whilſt he would violate his Mind, or perſecute his Body, for Matters of Faith or Worſhip towards his God.

Thus the *falſe Church* ſprang up, and mounted

ed the *Chair*: But though she lost her Nature, she would needs keep her good Name of the *Lamb's Bride*, the *true Church* and *Mother* of the *Faithful*: Constraining all to receive her Mark, either in their Forehead or Right Hand; that is, publickly or privately. But indeed and in Truth she was *Mystery Babylon*, the *Mother* of *Harlots*, *Mother* of those that, with all their *Show* and *Outside* of *Religion*, were adulterated and gone from the *Spirit*, *Nature* and *Life* of Christ, and grown *Vain*, *Worldly*, *Ambitious*, *Covetous*, *Cruel*, &c. which are the Fruits of the Flesh, and not of the Spirit.

Now it was, that the *true Church* fled into the *Wilderness*; that is, from *Superstition* and *Violence*, to a *retired, solitary*, and *lonely State*; hidden, and as it were, *out of Sight of Men*, though not *out of the World*. Which shows that her wonted Visibility was not essential to the Being of a true Church in the Judgment of the *Holy Ghost*; *she being as true a Church in the Wilderness, though not as visible and lustrious, as when she was in her former Splendor of Profession*. In this State many Attempts she made to return, but the Waters were yet too high, and her Way blocked up, and many of her excellent Children, in several Nations and Centuries, fell by the Cruelty of Superstition, because they would not *fall from their Faithfulness to the Truth*.

The last Age did set some Steps towards it, both as to *Doctrine*, *Worship*, and *Practice*. But *Practice* quickly failed; for Wickedness flow'd in a little Time, as well among the *Professors* of the *Reformation*, as those they reformed from; so that by the Fruits of Conversation they were

not

not to be distinguished. And the Children of the Reformers, if not the Reformers themselves, betook themselves, very early, to *Earthly Policy* and *Power*; to uphold and carry on their Reformation that had been begun with *spiritual Weapons*; which I have often thought, has been one of the greatest Reasons the Reformation made no better Progress, as to the *Life* and *Soul* of *Religion*. For whilst the Reformers were lowly and spiritually Minded, and trusted in God, look'd to Him, and lived in His Fear, and consulted not with Flesh and Blood, nor sought Deliverance in their own Way, there were daily added to the Church such as, one might reasonably say, should be saved: For they were not so careful to be safe from Persecution, as to be faithful and inoffensive under it: Being more concerned to spread the Truth by their Faith and Patience in *Tribulation*, than to get the Worldly Power out of their Hands that inflicted those Sufferings upon them: And it will be well if the Lord suffer them not to fall, by the very same Way they took to stand.

In *Doctrine* they were in some Things short; in other Things, to avoid one Extream, they ran into another: And for *Worship*, there was for the Generality, more of *Man* in it than of God. They owned the *Spirit*, *Inspiration* and *Revelation* indeed, and grounded their Separation and Reformation upon the Sense and Understanding they received from it, in the Reading of the Scriptures of Truth. And this was their Plea, the *Scripture* is the *Text*, the *Spirit* the *Interpreter*, and *that* to every one *for himself.*—

But

But yet there was too much of human Invention, Tradition and Art, that remained both in praying and preaching; and of Worldly Authority and Worldly Greatness in their Ministers; especially in this Kingdom, *Sweden*, *Denmark*, and some Parts of *Germany*. God was therefore pleased in *England* to shift us from Vessel to Vessel: And the next Remove *humbled* the Ministry, so that they were more strict in preaching, devout in praying, and zealous for keeping the Lord's Day, and catechising of Children and Servants, and repeating at Home in their Families, what they had heard in publick. But even as these grew into Power, they were not only for *whipping* some out, but others into the Temple: And they appeared *rigid in their Spirits*, rather than severe in their Lives, and more for a Party than for Piety: Which brought forth another People, that were yet more retired and select.

They would not *communicate* at large, or in common with others; but formed Churches among themselves of such as could give some Account of their Conversion, at least, of very promising Experiences, of the Work of God's Grace upon their Hearts; and under mutual Agreements and Covenants of Fellowship, they kept together. These People were somewhat of a softer Temper, and seemed to recommend Religion by the Charms of its Love, Mercy and Goodness, rather than by the Terrors of its Judgments and Punishments; by which the former Party would have awed People into Religion.

They also allowed *greater Liberty* to prophecy than

than those before them; for they admitted any Member to speak or pray, as well as their Pastor, whom they always chose, and not the civil Magistrate. If such found any Thing pressing upon them *to either Duty*, even without the *Distinction* of *Clergy* or *Laity*, Persons of any Trade had their Liberty, be it never so *low* and *mechanical*. But, alas! even these People suffered great Loss: For tasting of *Worldly Empire*, and the *Favour* of *Princes*, and the *Gain* that ensued, they degenerated but too much. For though they had cried down National Churches and Ministry, and Maintenance too, some of them when it was their own Turn to be tried, fell under the Weight of Worldly Honour and Advantage, got into profitable Parsonages too much, and outlived and contradicted their own Principles: And, which was yet worse, turned, some of them, *absolute Persecutors of other Men for* God's Sake, that but so lately came themselves out of the Furnace; which drove many a Step farther, and that was into the Water: *Another Baptism*, as believing they were not *scripturally baptized*; and hoping to find that Presence and Power of God in submitting to this Watry Ordinance, which they desired and wanted.

These People also made Profession of *neglecting*, if not *renouncing* and *censuring*, not only the *Necessity*, but *Use* of all *human Learning*, as to the *Ministry*; and all other Qualifications to it, besides the *Helps* and *Gifts* of the *Spirit* of God, and those natural and common to Men. And for a Time they seemed like *John* of old, *a burning and a shining Light to other Societies*.

They

They were very diligent, plain and serious; strong in Scripture and bold in Profession; bearing much Reproach and Contradiction. But that which others fell by, proved their Snare. For Worldly Power spoiled them too; who had enough of it to try them what they would do if they had more: And they rested also, too much upon their Watry Dispensation, instead of passing, on more fully to that of the *Fire* and *Holy Ghost*, which was *His Baptism who came with a Fan in his Hand, that He might thoroughly* (and not in Part only) *purge his Floor, and take away the Dross and the Tin of his People, and make a Man finer than Gold.* Withal they grew high, rough and self-righteous; opposing farther Attainment: Too much forgetting the Day of their Infancy and Littleness, which gave them something of a real Beauty; insomuch that many left them, and all visible Churches and Societies, and wandered up and down, as *Sheep* without a *Shepherd*, and as *Doves* without their *Mates*; seeking their *Beloved*, but could not find Him (as their Souls desired to know Him) whom their Souls loved above their *chiefest Joy*.

These People were called *Seekers* by some, and the *Family of Love* by others; because as they came to the Knowledge of one another, they sometimes met together, not formally to pray or preach at appointed Times or Places, in their own Wills, as in Times past they were accustomed to do; but waited together in *Silence*; and as any Thing rose in any one of their Minds that they thought favoured of a *divine Spring*, they sometimes spoke. But so it was, that some of them

them not keeping in *Humility*, and in the *Fear* of God, after the Abundance of Revelation, were exalted *above Measure*; and for Want of staying their Minds in an humble Dependence upon Him that opened their Understandings, to see *great Things* in his *Law*, they ran out in their own Imaginations, and mixing them with those divine Openings, brought forth a monstrous Birth, to the Scandal of those that feared God, and waited daily in the Temple, not made with Hands, for the Consolation of *Israel*; the *Jew* inward, and Circumcision in Spirit.

This People obtained the Name of *Ranters*, from their extravagant Discourses and Practices. For they interpreted Christ's fulfilling of the Law for us, to be a discharging of us from any Obligation and Duty the Law required of us, instead of the Condemnation of the Law for Sins past, upon Faith and Repentance: And that now it was no Sin to do that which before it was a Sin to commit; the slavish Fear of the Law being taken off by Christ, and all Things good that Man did, if he did but do them with the Mind and Persuasion that it was so. Insomuch that divers fell into gross and enormous Practices; pretending in Excuse thereof, that they could, *without Evil*, commit the same Act which was Sin in another to do; thereby distinguishing between the *Action* and the *Evil* of it, by the Direction of the Mind, and Intention in the doing of it: Which was to make Sin super-abound by the Aboundings of Grace, and to turn from the Grace of God into Wantonness, a securer Way of sinning than before: As if Christ came not to save us from our Sins, but in our Sins; not to take away Sin, but that we might sin more freely at His Cost, and with less Danger to ourselves. I say, this ensnared divers, and brought them to an utter and lamentable Loss as to their eternal State; and they grew very troublesome to the *better Sort* of *People*, and furnished the Looser with an Occasion to prophane.

CHAP. II.

Of the Rise of this PEOPLE, *their* fundamental Principle, *and* Doctrine, *and* Practice, *in Twelve Points resulting from it: Their* Progress *and* Sufferings: *An Expostulation with* England *thereupon.*

IT was about that very Time, as you may see in *George Fox*'s Annals, that the eternal, wise and good God, was pleased in His infinite Love to honour and visit this *benighted* and *bewildred Nation*, with His *glorious Day-spring from on high*; yea, with a most sure and certain Sound of the *Word* of *Light* and *Life*, through the Testimony of a *chosen Vessel*, to an effectual and blessed Purpose, can many Thousands say, *Glory be to the Name of the Lord for ever.*

For as it reached the Conscience, and broke the Heart, and brought many to a Sense and Search, so that which People had been vainly seeking *without*, with much Pains and Cost, they by this Ministry, found *within*, where it was they wanted what they sought for, *viz.* The *right Way* to *Peace with* God. For they were directed to the *Light*

of

of Jesus Christ *within them*, as the *Seed* and *Leaven of the Kingdom of* God; near all, because *in all*, and God's *Talent to all*: A faithful and true *Witness*, and *just Monitor* in *every Bosom*. The *Gift* and *Grace* of God, to Life and Salvation, that appears to all though few regard it. This the traditional *Christian*, conceited of himself, and strong in his own Will and Righteousness, overcome with *blind Zeal* and *Passion*, either despised as a *low* and *common* Thing, or opposed as a *Novelty*, under many hard Names, and opprobrious Terms, denying in his ignorant and angry Mind, any fresh Manifestations of God's Power and Spirit in Man, in these Days, tho' never more needed to make true *Christians*. Not unlike those *Jews* of old, that rejected the Son of God, at the very same Time that they blindly professed to wait for the Messiah to come; because, alas! he appeared not among them according to their carnal Mind and Expectation.

This brought forth many abusive Books, which filled the greater Sort with *Envy*, and lesser with *Rage*; and made the Way and Progress of this blessed Testimony *straight* and *narrow* indeed to those that received it. However, God owned His own Work, and this Testimony did *effectually* reach, gather, comfort and establish the *Weary* and *Heavy Laden*, the *Hungry* and *Thirsty*, the *Poor* and *Needy*, the *Mournful* and *Sick*, of many Maladies, that had spent all upon Physicians of no Value, and waited for Relief from Heaven; Help only from above: Seeing, upon a serious Trial of all Things, nothing else would do but Christ *Himself*; the *Light of His Countenance*, a *Touch of His Garment*, and *Help from His Hand*; who *cured* the poor Woman's

Woman's Issue, *raised* the *Centurion*'s Servant, the *Widow*'s Son, the *Ruler*'s Daughter, and *Peter*'s Mother: And like her, they no sooner felt His Power and Efficacy upon their Souls, but they gave up to obey Him in a *Testimony* to His Power; and that with *resigned* Wills and *faithful* Hearts, thro' all *Mockings, Contradictions, Confiscations, Beatings, Prisons,* and many other *Jeopardies* that attended them for His blessed Name's Sake.

And truly they were very many, and very great; so that in all human Probability they must have been swallowed up *quick* of the proud and boisterous Waves that swelled and beat against them, but that the God of all their tender Mercies was with them in His glorious Authority; so that the Hills often fled, and the Mountains melted before the Power that filled them; working mightily for them, as well as in them, one ever following the other. By which they saw plainly, to their exceeding great Confirmation and Comfort, that *all Things* were possible with Him with whom they had to do. And that the more that which God required seemed to cross Man's Wisdom, and expose them to Man's Wrath, the more God appeared to help and carry them through all to His Glory.

Insomuch, that if ever any People could say in Truth, Thou art our *Sun* and our *Shield*, our *Rock* and *Sanctuary*; and by Thee we have *leaped over a Wall*, and by Thee we have *run through a Troop*, and by thee we have put *put the Armies of the Aliens to flight*, these People had a Right to say it. And as God had delivered their Souls of the wearisom Burdens of Sin and Vanity, and enriched their Poverty of Spirit, and satisfied their great Hunger and

and Thirst after eternal Righteousness, and filled them with the good Things of His own House, and made them *Stewards* of His manifold Gifts; so they went forth to all Quarters of these Nations, to declare to the Inhabitants thereof, *what God had done for them; what they had found, and where and how they had found it, viz. The Way to Peace with God* : Inviting all to come, and see, and taste, for themselves, the Truth of what they declared unto them.

And as their Testimony was to the *Principle of God in Man,* the *precious Pearl* and *Leaven of the Kingdom*, as the only blessed Means appointed of God to quicken, convince and sanctify Man ; so they opened to them what it was in itself, and what it was given to them for : *How* they might know it from their own Spirit, and that of the subtle Appearance of the evil One : And what it would do for all those whose Minds should be turned off from the Vanity of the World, and its Lifeless Ways and Teachers, and adhere to His blessed Light in themselves, which discovers and condemns Sin in all its Appearances, and shews how to overcome it, if minded and obeyed in its holy Manifestations and Convictions : Giving Power to such to avoid and resist those Things that do not please God, and to grow strong in Love, Faith and good Works : That so Man, whom Sin hath made as a *Wilderness*, over-run with Briars and Thorns, might become as the *Garden* of God, cultivated by His divine Power, and replenished with the most virtuous and beautiful Plants of God's *own Right Hand planting,* to His eternal Praise.

But these experimental Preachers of glad Tidings

ings of God's Truth and Kingdom, could not run when they lift, or pray or preach when they pleased, but as Chrift their Redeemer *prepared* and *moved them by His own bleſſed Spirit*, for which they waited in their Services and Meetings, and ſpoke *as that gave them Utterance*; and which was as thoſe having Authority, and not like the dreaming dry and formal *Phariſees*. And ſo it plainly appeared to the Serious-minded, whoſe ſpiritual Eye the Lord Jeſus had in any Meaſure opened: So that to one was given the Word of *Exhortation*, to another the Word of *Reproof*, to another the Word of *Conſolation*, and all by the ſame Spirit and in the good Order thereof, to the convincing and edifying of many.

And truly they waxed ſtrong and bold through Faithfulneſs; and by the Power and Spirit of the Lord Jeſus became very fruitful; Thouſands, in a ſhort Time, being turned to the Truth in the inward Parts through their Teſtimony in *Miniſtry* and *Sufferings*: Inſomuch as in moſt Counties, and many of the conſiderable Towns of *England*, Meetings were ſettled, and daily there were added ſuch as ſhould be ſaved. For they were diligent to *plant* and to *water*, and the Lord bleſſed their Labours with an *exceeding great Increaſe*; notwithſtanding all the Oppoſition made to their bleſſed Progreſs, by *falſe Rumours, Calumnies* and *bitter Perſecutions*; not only from the *Powers* of the Earth, but from every one that liſted to injure and abuſe them: So that they ſeemed indeed to be as *poor Sheep* appointed to the *Slaughter*, and as a *People killed all the Day long.*

It were fitter for a *Volume* than a *Preface*, but ſo much

much as to repeat the *Contents* of their cruel Sufferings from *Profeſſors* as well as from *Prophane*, and from *Magiſtrates* as well as the *Rabble*: That it may be ſaid of this abuſed and deſpiſed People, they went forth *weeping* and ſowed in *Tears*, bearing Teſtimony to the *precious Seed*, even the *Seed* of the *Kingdom*, which ſtands not in *Words*; the fineſt, the higheſt that Man's Wit can uſe, but in *Power*: The Power of Chriſt Jeſus, to whom God the Father hath given *all Power* in Heaven and in Earth, that He might rule *Angels* above, and *Men* below. Who impowered them, as their Work witneſſeth, by the many that were *turned*, through their Miniſtry, from *Darkneſs* to the *Light*, and out of the *broad* into the *narrow Way* of Life and Peace; bringing People to a weighty, ſerious and God-like Converſation; the *Practice* of that *Doctrine* which they taught.

And as without this ſecret *divine Power* there is no *quickening* and *regenerating* of *dead Souls*, ſo the Want of this *generating* and *begetting* Power and Life, is the Cauſe of the little Fruit that the many Miniſtries, that have been and are in the World, bring forth. O that both Miniſters and People were ſenſible of this! My Soul is often troubled for them, and Sorrow and Mourning compaſs me about for their Sakes. O that they were wiſe! O that they would conſider, and lay to Heart the Things that truly and ſubſtantially make for their laſting Peace!

Two Things are to be conſidered, the *Doctrine* they taught, and the *Example* they led among all People. I have already touched upon their *fundamental Principle*, which is as the *Corner-Stone* of
their

their Fabrick: And indeed, to speak eminently and properly, their *Characteristick*, or main distinguishing Point or Principle, *viz.* The *Light of Christ within*, as God's Gift for Man's Salvation. This, I say, is as the *Root* of the goodly Tree of Doctrines that grew and branched out from it, which I shall now mention in their natural and experimental Order.

First, *Repentance from Dead Works to serve the living* God. Which comprehends three Operations. First, a *Sight* of Sin. Secondly, a *Sense* and *Godly Sorrow* for Sin. Thirdly, an *Amendment for the Time to come.* This was the Repentance they preached and pressed, and a natural Result from the Principle they turned all People unto. For of *Light* came *Sight*; and of *Sight* came *Sense* and *Sorrow*; and of *Sense* and *Sorrow* came *Amendment of Life.* Which Doctrine of Repentance leads to *Justification*; that is, *Forgiveness of the Sins that are past, through* Christ *the alone Propitiation, and the Sanctification or Purgation of the Soul,* from the defiling Nature and Habits of Sin *present*, by the Spirit of Christ in the Soul; which is Justification in the compleat Sense of that Word: Comprehending both Justification from the *Guilt* of the Sins that are past, as if they had never been committed, through the Love and Mercy of God in Christ Jesus; and the Creature's being made inwardly just through the *cleansing* and *sanctifying* Power and Spirit of Christ revealed in the Soul; which is commonly called *Sanctification.* But that none can come to know Christ to be their Sacrifice that reject Him as their Sanctifier: The End of His Coming being to save His People from the

the *Nature* and *Defilement*, as well as *Guilt* of Sin; and that therefore thofe that refift His Light and Spirit, make His Coming and Offering of none Effect to them.

From hence fprang a *fecond Doctrine* they were led to declare, as the *Mark of the Price of the high Calling* to all true *Chriftians*, viz. *Perfection from Sin*, according to the Scriptures of Truth; which teftify it to be the *End* of Chrift's Coming, and the *Nature* of His Kingdom, and for which His Spirit was and is given, viz. To be *perfect as our Heavenly Father is perfect*, and *holy, becaufe God is holy*. And this the Apoftles laboured for, *That the* Chriftians *fhould be fanctified throughout in Body, Soul and Spirit*; but they never held a Perfection in *Wifdom* and *Glory* in this Life, or from *natural Infirmities*, or Death, as fome have, with a weak or ill Mind, imagined and infinuated againft them.

This they called a *redeemed State, Regeneration*, or the *new Birth:* Teaching every where according to their *Foundation*, that unlefs this Work was known, there was no inheriting the Kingdom of God.

Thirdly, This leads to an Acknowledgment of *eternal Rewards* and *Punifhments*, as they have good Reafon; for elfe, of all People, certainly they muft be *moft miferable;* who, for above *forty* Years, have been exceeding great Sufferers for their Profeffion; and in fome Cafes, treated *worfe* than the *worft* of Men; yea, as the *Refufe* and *Offscouring* of all Things.

This was the *Support* of their *Doctrine* and *Miniftry;* which, for the moft Part, is what other Profeffors

fors of *Christianity* pretend to hold in Words and Forms, but not in the Power of Godliness; which, generally speaking, has been long lost by Men's departing from that *Principle* and *Seed of Life* that is in Man, and which Man has not regarded, but lost the Sense of; and in and by which he can *only* be quickened in his Mind to serve the living God in *Newness* of Life. For as the Life of Religion was lost, and the Generality lived and worshipped God after their own Wills, and not after the Will of God, nor the Mind of Christ, which stood in the Works and Fruits of the *holy Spirit*; so that which they prest, was not *Notion*, but *Experience*; not *Formality*, but *Godliness*; as being sensible in themselves, through the Work of God's righteous Judgments, that *without Holiness no Man shall ever see the* Lord with Comfort.

Besides these *general Doctrines*, as the larger Branches, there sprang forth several *particular Doctrines*, that did *exemplify* and *farther explain* the Truth and Efficacy of the *general Doctrine* before observed, in their *Lives* and *Examples*. As,

I. *Communion and loving one another.* This is a noted Mark in the Mouth of all Sorts of People concerning them. *They will meet, they will help and stick one to another.* Whence it is common to hear some say, *Look how the* Quakers *love and take care of one another.* Others less moderate, will say, *The* Quakers *love none but themselves*: And if *loving* one another, and if having an *intimate Communion* in Religion, and *constant Care* to meet to worship God, and help one another, be any Mark of *primitive Christianity*, they had it, blessed be the Lord, in an ample Manner.

II. *To*

II. *To love Enemies.* This they both *taught* and *practised.* For they did not only refuse to be revenged for Injuries done them, and condemned it as of an unchristian Spirit; but they did *freely forgive*, yea, *help* and *relieve* those that had been *cruel* to them, when it was in their Power to have been even with them: Of which many and singular Instances might be given: Endeavouring, through Faith and Patience, to overcome all Injustice and Oppression, and preaching this Doctrine as *Christian*, for others to follow.

III. Another was, *The Sufficiency of Truth-speaking*, according to Christ's own Form of sound Words, of *Yea, Yea,* and *Nay, Nay,* among *Christians, without swearing*; both from Christ's express Prohibition, to *swear at all,* Mat. v. and for that they being under the Tye and Bond of Truth in themselves, there was no Necessity for an Oath; and it would be a Reproach to their *Christian* Veracity to assure their Truth by such an extraordinary Way of speaking; simple and uncompound Answers, as *Yea* and *Nay*, (without Asseveration, Attestation, or supernatural Vouchers) being most suitable to Evangelical Righteousness. But offering at the same Time to be punished to the full, for *False-speaking*, as others for *Perjury*, if ever guilty of it: And hereby they exclude with all true, all *false* and *prophane swearing*; for which the Land did and doth *mourn*, and the great God was, and is not a little offended with it.

IV. *Not Fighting, but Suffering,* is another Testimony peculiar to this People: They affirm that *Christianity* teacheth People *to beat their Swords into*

into *Plough-shares, and their Spears into Pruning-hooks, and to learn War no more,* that so the Wolf may lie down with the Lamb, and the Lyon with the Calf; and nothing, that destroys, be entertained in the Hearts of People: Exhorting them to employ their Zeal against *Sin,* and turn their Anger against *Satan,* and no longer war one against another; because *all Wars and Fightings come of Men's own Hearts Lusts,* according to the Apostle *James,* and not of the meek Spirit of Christ Jesus, who is Captain of *another Warfare,* and which is carried on with *other Weapons.* Thus, as *Truth-speaking* succeeded *Swearing, so Faith* and *Patience* succeeded *Fighting,* in the Doctrine and Practice of this People. Nor ought they for this to be obnoxious to Civil Government, since if they cannot *fight for it, neither can they fight against it*; which is no mean Security to any State. Nor is it reasonable that People should be blamed for not doing more for others than they can do for themselves. And, *Christianity* set aside, if the Costs and Fruits of War were well considered, Peace, with all its Inconveniencies, is generally preferable. But though they were not for *fighting,* they were for *submitting* to Government; and that, not only for *Fear, but for* Conscience-sake; where Government doth not *interfere* with Conscience; believing it to be an Ordinance of God, and where it is justly administred, a great Benefit to Mankind. Though it has been their Lot, through blind Zeal in some, and Interest in others, to have felt the *Strokes* of it with greater Weight and Rigour than any other Perswasion in this Age; whilst they of all others, *Religion* set aside, have given the Civil Magistrate

Magistrate the least Occasion of Trouble in the Discharge of his Office.

V. Another Part of the *Character* of this People was, and is, *They refuse to pay Tithes or Maintenance to a* National Ministry; and that for two Reasons: The one is, they believe all *compelled* Maintenance, even to Gospel-Ministers, to be *unlawful*, because expressly contrary to Christ's Command, who said, *Freely you have received, freely give:* At least, that the Maintenance of Gospel-Ministers should be free, and not forced. The other Reason of their Refusal is, because those Ministers are not *Gospel Ones,* in that the Holy Ghost is not their Foundation, but human *Arts* and *Parts.* So that it is not Matter of Humour or Sullenness, but *pure Conscience* towards God, that they cannot help to support *National Ministries* where they dwell, which are but too much and too visible become Ways of Worldly Advantage and Preferment.

VI. *Not to respect Persons*, was, and is another of their Doctrines and Practices, for which they were often *buffetted* and *abused*. They affirmed it to be sinful to give *flattering Titles*, or to use *vain Gestures* and *Compliments* of *Respect*. Though to *Virtue* and *Authority* they ever made a *Difference*; but after their plain and homely Manner, yet sincere and substantial Way: Well remembring the Examples of *Mordecai* and *Elihu*; but more especially the Command of their Lord and Master Jesus Christ, who forbad His Followers to call Men *Rabbi*, which implies *Lord* or *Master*; also the *fashionable Greetings* and *Salutations* of those Times; that so *Self-Love* and *Honour*, to which the proud

C   Mind

Mind of Man is incident, in his fallen Estate, might not be indulged but rebuked. And though this rendered their Conversation disagreeable, yet they that will remember what Christ said to the *Jews, How can you believe which receive Honour one of another*, will abate of their Resentment, if His Doctrine has any Credit with them.

VII. They also used the plain Language of *Thee* and *Thou*, to a single Person, whatever was his Degree among Men. And indeed the Wisdom of God was much seen, in bringing forth this People in so plain an Appearance. For it was a *close* and *distinguishing Test* upon the Spirits of those they came among; shewing their Insides, and what predominated, notwithstanding their high and great Profession of Religion. This among the rest sounded so harsh to many of them, and they took it so ill, that they would say, *Thou me, thou my Dog! If thou thou'st me, I'll thou thy Teeth down thy Throat*; forgetting the Language *they use to* God in their own Prayers, and the common Stile of the Scriptures, and that it is an absolute and essential Propriety of Speech. And what good, alas! had their Religion done them, who were so sensibly touched with Indignity for the Use of this *plain, honest* and *true Speech?*

VIII. They recommended *Silence* by their Example, having very few Words upon all Occasions. They were *at a Word* in Dealing: Nor could their Customers, with many Words tempt them from it, having more Regard to *Truth* than *Custom*, to *Example* than *Gain*. They sought *Solitude*; but when in Company, they would neither use, nor willingly hear *unnecessary* or *unlawful* Discourses:

courses: Whereby they preserved their Minds *pure* and *undisturbed* from unprofitable Thoughts, and Diversions. Nor could they humour the Custom of *Good Night, Good Morrow, God Speed*; for they knew the Night was good, and the Day was good, without wishing of either; and that in the other Expression, the holy Name of God was too lightly and unthankfully used, and therefore taken in vain. Besides, they were Words and Wishes of Course, and are usually as little meant, as are Love and Service in the Custom of *Cap* and *Knee*; and Superfluity in those, as well as in other Things, was burthensome to them; and therefore they did not only decline to use them, but found themselves often pressed to reprove the Practice.

IX. For the same Reason they *forbore drinking to People*, or *pledging of them*, as the Manner of the World is: A Practice that is not only unnecessary, but they thought Evil in the *Tendencies* of it, being a *Provocation* to drink more than did People good, as well as that it was in itself *vain* and *Heathenish*.

X. Their Way of *Marriage* is peculiar to them; and shews a distinguishing Care, above other Societies, professing *Christianity*. They say that *Marriage is an Ordinance of God*, and *that God only can rightly join Man and Woman in Marriage:* Therefore they use neither *Priest* nor *Magistrate*; but the Man and Woman concerned, take each other as Husband and Wife, in the Presence of divers credible Witnesses, *promising to each other, with God's Assistance, to be loving and faithful in that Relation, till Death shall seperate them*. But antece-

antecedent to this, they first present themselves to the *Monthly Meeting*, for the Affairs of the Church where they reside; there declaring their Intentions, to take one another as Husband and Wife, if the said Meeting have nothing material to object against it. They are constantly asked the necessary Questions, as in case of *Parents* or *Guardians*, if they have acquainted them with their Intention, and have their Consent, &c. The Method of the Meeting is, to take a Minute thereof, and to appoint proper Persons to enquire of their Conversation and Clearness from all others, and whether they have discharged their Duty to their *Parents* or *Guardians*; and to make Report thereof to the next *Monthly Meeting*, where the same Parties are desired to give their Attendance. In case it appears they have proceeded orderly, the Meeting passes their Proposal, and so records it in their *Meeting-Book*. And in case the Woman be a Widow, and hath Children, due Care is there taken, that Provision also be made by her for the *Orphans*, before the Meeting pass the Proposals of Marriage: Advising the Parties concerned, to appoint a convenient Time and Place, and to give fitting Notice to their Relations, and such Friends and Neighbours, as they desire should be the Witnesses of their Marriage: Where they take one another by the Hand, and by Name promise reciprocally, Love and Fidelity, after the Manner before expressed. Of all which Proceedings, a Narrative, in Way of Certificate, is made, to which the said Parties first set their Hands, thereby confirming it as their Act and Deed; and then divers Relations, Spectators and Auditors, set their

their Names as Witnesses, of what they said and signed. And this Certificate is afterwards registred in the Record belonging to the Meeting where the Marriage is solemnized. Which regular Method has been, as it deserves, adjudged in Courts of Law, a *good Marriage*; where it has been by cross and ill People disputed, and contested, for Want of the accustomed Formalities of *Priest* and *Ring*, &c. Ceremonies they have refused: Not out of Humour, but Conscience reasonably grounded; inasmuch as no Scripture-Example tells us, that the Priest had any other Part of old Time, than that of a Witness among the rest, before whom the *Jews* used to take one another: And therefore this People look upon it as an Imposition to advance the Power and Profits of the Clergy: And for the Use of the *Ring*, it is enough to say, that it was an *Heathenish* and vain Custom, and never in Practice among the People of God, *Jews* or primitive *Christians*: The Words of the usual Form, as *with my Body I thee worship*, &c. are hardly defensible. In short, they are more careful, exact and regular, than any Form now used; and it is free of the Inconveniencies, with which other Methods are attended: Their Care and Checks being so many, and such, as that no *clandestine Marriages* can be performed among them.

X. It may not be unfit to say something here of their *Births* and *Burials*, which make up so much of the Pomp of too many called *Christians*. For *Births*, the Parents name their own Children; which is usually some Days after they are born, in the Presence of the Midwife, if she can be there, and

and those that were at the Birth, who afterwards sign a Certificate for that Purpose prepared, of the Birth and Name of the Child or Children; which is recorded in a proper Book, in the *Monthly Meeting* to which the Parents belong; avoiding the accustomed Ceremonies and Festivals.

XI. Their *Burials* are performed with the same Simplicity. If the Body of the Deceased be near any publick Meeting-Place, it is usually carried thither, for the more convenient Reception of those that accompany it to the Burying-Ground. And it so falls out sometimes, that while the Meeting is gathering for the Burial, some or other has a Word of Exhortation, for the Sake of the People there met together. After which the Body is borne away by young Men, or else those that are of their Neighbourhood, or those that were most of the Intimacy of the deceased Party: The Corps being in a *plain Coffin, without any Covering or Furniture* upon it. At the Ground, they pause some Time before they put the Body into its Grave, that if any there should have any Thing upon them to exhort the People, they may not be disappointed; and that the Relations may the more retiredly and solemnly take their last Leave of the Body of their departed Kindred, and the Spectators have a Sense of Mortality, by the Occasion then given them, to reflect upon their own latter End. Otherwise, they have no set Rites or Ceremonies on those Occasions. Neither do the Kindred of the Deceased ever wear *Mourning*†; they looking upon

---

† N. B. Since the Time this Account was first published, *(Anno 1694)* some of the Posterity of this People have visibly degenerated from

upon it as a Worldly Ceremony and Piece of Pomp; and that what Mourning is fit for a *Christian* to have, at the Departure of a beloved Relation or Friend, should be worn in the Mind, which is only sensible of the Loss: And the Love they had to them, and Remembrance of them, to be outwardly expressed by a Respect to their Advice, and Care of those they have left behind them, and their Love of that they loved. Which Conduct of theirs, though unmodish or unfashionable, leaves nothing of the Substance of Things neglected or undone: And as they Aim at no more, so that Simplicity of Life is what they observe with great Satisfaction; though it sometimes happens not to be without the Mockeries of the vain World they live in.

These Things to be sure gave them a rough and disagreeable Appearance with the Generality; who thought them *Turners of the World upside down*, as indeed, in some Sense they were: But in no other than that wherein *Paul* was so charged, viz. *To bring Things back into their primitive and right Order again.* For these and such like Practices of theirs were not the Result of Humour, or for *Civil Distinction*, as some have fancied, but a Fruit of *inward Sense*, which God, through His holy Fear, had begotten in them. They did not consider how to contradict the World, or distinguish themselves as a Party from others; it being

from the primitive Plainness of their Predecessors in this Respect; nevertheless, the collective Sense and Judgment of the Church herein, remains the same, as is manifest by the frequent Advices given forth from their Yearly and other Meetings.

none of their Business, as it was not their Interest: No, it was not the Result of Consultation or a framed Design, by which to declare or recommend Schism or Novelty. But God having given them a Sight of themselves, they saw the whole World in the *same Glass of Truth*; and sensibly discerned the Affections and Passions of Men, and the Rise and Tendency of Things: What it was that gratified the *Lust of the Flesh, the Lust of the Eye, and the Pride of Life, which are not of the Father, but of the World*. And from thence sprang in the Night of Darkness and Apostacy which hath been over People through their Degeneration from the Light and Spirit of God, these and many other vain Customs, which are seen by the heavenly Day of Christ, *that dawns in the Soul*, to be, either wrong in their *Original*; or, by Time and Abuse, hurtful in their *Practice*. And though these Things seemed trivial to some, and rendered these People stingy and conceited in such Persons Opinion; there was and is more in them, than they were, or are aware of.

It was not very easy to our *primitive Friends* to make themselves *Sights* and *Spectacles*, and the *Scorn* and *Derision* of the World; which they easily foresaw must be the Consequence of so *unfashionable* a Conversation in it: But here was the Wisdom of God seen in the Foolishness of these Things; *first*, That they discovered the *Satisfaction* and *Concern* that People had in and for the Fashions of this World, notwithstanding their high Pretences to another; in that any Disappointment about them came so very near them, as that the greatest Honesty, Virtue, Wisdom and Ability, ty, were *unwelcome* without them. *Secondly*, It *seasonably* and *profitably divided Conversation*; for this making their Society uneasy to their Relations and Acquaintance, it gave them the Opportunity of *more Retirement* and *Solitude*; wherein they met with better Company, even the Lord God *their Redeemer*; and grew strong in His Love, Power and Wisdom, and were thereby better qualified for His Service. And the Success abundantly show'd it: *Blessed be the Name of the Lord*.

And though they were not great and learned in the Esteem of this World, (for then they had not wanted Followers upon their own Credit and Authority) yet they were generally of the *most sober* of the several Persuasions they were in, and of the *most Repute* for Religion; and many of them of *good Capacity, Substance* and *Account* among Men.

And also some among them wanted not for *Parts, Learning* or *Estate*; tho' then as of old, *not many Wise,* or *Noble,* &c. *were called*; or at least received the *Heavenly Call*, because of the Cross that attended the Profession of it in Sincerity. But neither do Parts or Learning make Men the better *Christians*, though the better Orators and Disputants; and it is the Ignorance of People about the divine Gift that causes that vulgar and mischievous Mistake. *Theory* and *Practice, Speculation* and *Enjoyment, Words* and *Life,* are two Things. O 'tis the Penitent, the Reformed, the Lowly, the Watchful, the Self-denying and holy Soul, that is the *Christian!* And that Frame is the Fruit and Work of the *Spirit*, which is the Life of Jesus: Whose Life though hid

hid in the Fulness of it in God the Father, is shed abroad in the Hearts of them that truly believe, according to their Capacity. O that People did but know this to cleanse them, to circumcise them, to quicken them, and to make them *new Creatures* indeed! *Recreated* or *Regenerated* after Christ Jesus unto good Works; that they might live to God, and not to themselves; *and offer up living Prayers and living Praises, to the living God, through His own living Spirit,* in which He is only to be worshipped in this Gospel Day.

O that they that read me could but feel me! For my Heart is affected with this *merciful Visitation* of the Father of Lights and Spirits to this poor Nation, and the whole World, through the same Testimony. Why should the Inhabitants thereof *reject* it? Why should they lose the blessed Benefit of it? Why should they not *turn to the Lord with all their Hearts,* and say from the Heart, *speak Lord, for now Thy poor Servants hear? O that Thy Will may be done; Thy great, Thy good and holy Will, in Earth as it is in Heaven!* Do it in us, do it upon us, do what Thou wilt with us; *for we are Thine, and desire to glorify Thee our* Creator, *both for that, and because Thou art our* Redeemer; *for Thou art redeeming us from the Earth; from the Vanities and Pollutions of it, to be a peculiar People unto Thee.* O this were a brave Day for *England,* if so she could say in Truth! But alas, the Case is otherwise; for which some of thine Inhabitants, O Land of my Nativity! have mourned over thee with *bitter Wailing* and *Lamentation.* Their Heads have been indeed as Waters, and their Eyes as Fountains of Tears, because of thy Transgression and

Stiff-neckedness; because thou wilt not hear, and fear, and return to the *Rock*, even *thy Rock*, O *England!* From whence thou art hewn. But be thou warned, O Land of great Profession, to receive Him into thy Heart. Behold *at that Door* it is He hath stood so long knocking! but thou wilt yet have none of Him. O be thou awakened, lest *Jerusalem*'s Judgments do swiftly overtake thee, because of *Jerusalem*'s Sins that abound in thee. For she abounded in *Formality*, but made void the weighty Things of God's Law, as thou daily doft.

She withstood the Son of God *in the Flesh*, and thou resisteft the Son of God *in the Spirit*. He would have gathered her as an Hen gathereth her Chickens under her Wings, and she would not; *so would He have gathered thee out of thy* Lifeless *Profession, and have brought thee to inherit* Substance; to have known His Power and Kingdom: For which He often knocked within, by His *Grace* and *Spirit*; and without, by His *Servants* and *Witnesses:* But on the Contrary, as *Jerusalem* of old persecuted the Manifestation of the Son of God in the Flesh, and *crucified Him*, and *whipt* and *imprisoned* His Servants; so hast thou, O Land! crucified *to thyself afresh* the Lord of Life and Glory, and done *Despite* to His Spirit of Grace; *slighting* the Fatherly Visitation, and persecuting the blessed Dispensers of it by thy Laws and Magistrates: Though they have early and late pleaded with thee in the *Power* and *Spirit* of the Lord; in *Love* and *Meekness*, that thou mightest know the Lord, and serve Him, and become the Glory of all Lands.

But

But thou haſt evilly entreated and requited them, thou *haſt ſet at nought* all their Counſel, and *would'ſt have none* of their Reproof, as thou ſhould'ſt have had. Their Appearance was *too ſtrait*, and their Qualifications were *too mean* for thee to receive them; like the *Jews*, of old, that cried, *Is not this the* Carpenter's Son, *and are not his Brethren among us; which of the Scribes, of the Learned* (the Orthodox) *believe in Him?* Propheſying their Fall in a Year or two, and making and executing of ſevere Laws to bring it to paſs: Endeavouring to terrify them out of their *holy Way*, or deſtroy them for abiding faithful to it. But thou haſt ſeen how many Governments that roſe againſt them, and determined their downfal, have been overturned and extinguiſhed, and that they are ſtill preſerved, and become a great and conſiderable People, among the middle Sort of thy numerous Inhabitants. And notwithſtanding the many Difficulties without and within, which they have laboured under, ſince the Lord God Eternal firſt gathered them, they are an encreaſing People; the Lord ſtill adding unto them, in divers Parts, ſuch as ſhall be ſaved, if they perſevére to the End. And to thee, O *England!* were they, and are they lifted up as a Standard, and as a City ſet upon an Hill, and to the Nations round about thee, that *in their Light thou may'ſt come to ſee Light*, even in Chriſt Jeſus, *the Light of the World*, and therefore *thy Light, and Life too*, if thou would'ſt but turn from thy many evil Ways, and receive and obey it. *For in the Light of the Lamb muſt the Nations of them that are ſaved walk*, as the Scripture teſtifies.

Remember,

Remember, O Nation of great Profession! how the Lord has waited upon thee since the Dawning Reformation, and the many Mercies and Judgments by which He has pleaded with thee; and awake and arise out of thy deep Sleep, and yet hear his Word *in thy Heart*, that thou may'st live.

Let not this thy Day of Visitation pass over thy Head, nor neglect thou so great Salvation as is this which is come to thy House, O *England!* for, why should'st thou die? O Land that God desires to bless! Be assured *it is He* that has been in the Midst of *this People*, in the Midst of thee, and not a Delusion, as thy mistaken Teachers have made thee believe. And this thou shalt find by their Marks and Fruits, if thou wilt consider them in the Spirit of Moderation.

CHAP. III.

Of the Qualifications of their Ministry.

Eleven Marks that it is Christian.

I. THEY were *changed Men themselves* before they went about to change others. Their *Hearts were rent* as well as their Garments; and they knew the Power and Work of God upon them. And this was seen by the great Alteration it made, and their stricter Course of Life, and more Godly Conversation that immediately followed upon it.

II. They went not forth, or preached in their own Time or Will, but in the *Will of God*; and spoke

spoke not their own studied Matters, but as they were opened and moved of His Spirit, with which they were well acquainted in their own Conversion: Which cannot be expressed to carnal Men, so as to give them any intelligible Account; for to such it is, as Christ said, like the blowing of the Wind, which no Man knows, whence it cometh, or whither it goeth: Yet this Proof and Seal went along with their Ministry, that many were turned from their Lifeless Professions, and the Evil of their Ways, to an inward and experimental Knowledge of God, and an holy Life, as Thousands can witness. And as they *freely* received what they had to say from the Lord, so they *freely* administred it to others.

III. The Bent and Stress of their Ministry was *Conversion* to God; *Regeneration* and *Holiness*. Not Schemes of Doctrines and verbal Creeds, or new Forms of Worship; but a leaving off in Religion the superfluous, and reducing the ceremonious and formal Part, and pressing earnestly the *substantial*, the *necessary* and *profitable* Part to the Soul; as all, upon a serious Reflection, must and do acknowledge.

IV. They directed People to a *Principle* in themselves, though not of themselves, by which all that they asserted, preached and exhorted others to, might be wrought in them, and known to them, through Experience, to be true: Which is an high and distinguishing Mark of the Truth of their Ministry, both that they knew what they said, and were not afraid of coming to the Test. For as they were bold from Certainty, so they required Conformity upon no human Authority, but

but upon *Conviction*, and the Conviction of *this Principle*, which they afferted was in them that they preached unto; and unto that they directed them, that they might examine and prove the Reality of those Things which they had affirmed of it, as to its Manifeftation and Work in Man. And this is more than the many Minifters in the World pretended to. They declare of Religion, fay many Things true, in Words, of God, Chrift, and the *Spirit*; of *Holinefs* and *Heaven*; that all Men fhould *repent* and *amend* their Lives, or they will go to *Hell*, &c. But which of them all pretend to fpeak of *their own Knowledge and Experience?* Or ever directed to a divine Principle, or Agent, placed of God *in Man*, to help him; and how to know it, and wait to feel its Power to work that good and acceptable Will of God in them.

Some of them indeed have fpoke of the *Spirit*, and the Operations of it to Sanctification, and Performance of Worfhip to God; but *where* and *how* to find it, and wait in it, to perform our Duty to God, was yet as a Myftery to be declared by this farther Degree of *Reformation*. So that this People did not only in Words, more than equally prefs *Repentance*, *Converfion*, and *Holinefs*, but did it knowingly and experimentally; and directed thofe, to whom they preached, to a fufficient Principle; and told them where it was, and by what Tokens they might know it, and which Way they might experience the Power and Efficacy of it to their Souls Happinefs. Which is more than *Theory* and *Speculation*, upon which moft other Minifters depend: For here is *Certainty*;
a Bottom

a Bottom upon which Man may boldly appear before God in the great Day of Account.

V. They reached to the inward State and Condition of People, which is an Evidence of the Virtue of their Principle, and of their Ministring from it, and not from their own Imaginations, Glosses, or Comments upon Scripture. For nothing reaches the Heart, but what is *from the Heart*, or pierces the Conscience, but what comes from a *living Conscience:* Insomuch as it hath often happened, where People have under Secrecy revealed their State or Condition to some choice Friends, for Advice or Ease, they have been so particularly directed in the Ministry of this People, that they have challenged their Friends with discovering their Secrets, and telling their preachers their Cases, to whom a Word had not been spoken. Yea, the very Thoughts and Purposes of the Hearts of many have been so plainly detected, that they have, like *Nathaniel*, cried out, of this inward Appearance of Christ, *Thou art the Son of God, Thou art the King of* Israel. And those that have embraced this divine Principle have found this Mark of its Truth and Divinity (that the Woman of *Samaria* did of Christ when in the Flesh, to be the Messiah) viz. *It had told them all that ever they had done*; shown them their Insides, the most inward Secrets of their Hearts, and laid Judgment to the Line, and Righteousness to the Plummet; of which Thousands, can at this Day, give in their Witness. So that nothing has been affirmed by this People, of the Power and Virtue of this Heavenly Principle, that such as have turned to it have not found true, and more; and that one
half

half had not been told them of what they have seen of the *Power*, *Purity*, *Wisdom* and *Goodness* of God therein.

VI. The *Accomplishments* with which this Principle fitted, even some of the Meanest of this People, for their Work and Service: Furnishing some of them with an extraordinary Understanding in divine Things, and an admirable Fluency and Taking Way of Expression, which gave Occasion to some to wonder, saying of them, as of their Master, *Is not this such a Mechanick's Son, how came he by this Learning?* As from thence others took Occasion to suspect and insinuate they were *Jesuits* in Disguise, (who had the Reputation of learned Men for an Age past,) tho' there was not the least Ground of Truth for any such Reflection. In that their Ministers are known, the Places of their Abode, their Kindred and Education.

VII. That they came forth *low*, and *despised* and *hated*, as the primitive *Christians* did, and not by the Help of Worldly Wisdom or Power, as former Reformations in Part, have done: But in all Things it may be said, this People were brought forth in the *Cross*; in a *Contradiction* to the *Ways*, *Worships*, *Fashions* and *Customs* of this *World*; yea, against *Wind* and *Tide*, that so no Flesh might glory before God.

VIII. They could have *no Design to themselves in this Work*, thus to expose themselves to *Scorn and Abuse*; to spend and be spent: Leaving *Wife* and *Children*, *House* and *Land*, and all that can be accounted dear to Men, with their Lives in their Hands, being daily in Jeopardy, to declare this

primitive

primitive Message, revived in their Spirits, by the good Spirit and Power of God, *viz.*

That God *is Light and in Him is no Darkness at all; and that He has sent His Son a Light into the World, to Enlighten all Men in order to Salvation; and that they that say they have Fellowship with* God, *and are his Children and People, and yet walk in Darkness,* viz. *in Disobedience to the Light in their Consciences, and after the Vanity of this World,* they Lie, *and do not the Truth. But that all such as love the Light, and bring their Deeds to it, and walk in the Light, as* God *is Light, the Blood of* Jesus Christ *His Son, should cleanse them from all Sin.* Thus *John* i. 4, 19. Chap iii. 20, 21. 1 *John* i. 5, 6, 7.

IX. Their known great Constancy and Patience in suffering for their Testimony, in all the Branches of it; and that sometimes unto *Death,* by *Beatings, Bruisings, long* and *crowded Imprisonments,* and *noisome Dungeons:* Four of them in *New-England* dying by the Hands of the *Executioner,* purely for *Preaching* amongst *that People:* Besides *Banishments,* and *excessive Plunders* and *Sequestration,* of their *Goods* and *Estates,* almost in all Parts, not easily to be expressed, and less to have been endured, but by those that have the Support of a *good* and *glorious Cause;* refusing Deliverance by any indirect Ways or Means, as often as it was offered unto them.

X. That they did, not only, not show any Disposition to *Revenge,* when it was at any Time in their Power, but forgave their cruel Enemies; *shewing Mercy to those that had none for them.*

XI.

XI. Their *Plainness* with those in Authority, like the Ancient Prophets, not fearing to tell them to their Faces, of their private and public Sins; and their Prophecies to them of their Afflictions and Downfal, when in the Top of their Glory. Also of some National Judgments, as of the *Plague*, and *Fire* of *London*, in express Terms; and likewise particular ones to divers Persecutors, which accordingly overtook them; and were very remarkable in the Places where they dwelt, which in Time may be made publick for the Glory of God.

Thus, *Reader*, thou seest *this People* in their *Rise*, *Principles*, *Ministry* and *Progress*, both their *general* and *particular Testimony*; by which thou may'st be informed *how*, and *upon what Foot they sprang*, and *became so considerable a People*. It remains next, that I shew also their *Care*, *Conduct* and *Discipline*, as a *Christian* and *reformed Society*, that they might be found living up to their own *Principles* and *Profession*. And this, the rather, because they have hardly suffered more in their *Character* from the unjust Charge of *Error*, than by the false Imputation of *Disorder*; Which *Calumny* indeed has not failed to follow all the *true Steps* that were ever made to *Reformation*, and under which *Reproach* none suffered more than the *primitive Christians* themselves, that were the *Honour* of *Christianity*, and the *great Lights* and *Examples* of their own and succeeding Ages.

Of the Discipline *and* Practice *of this* PEOPLE, *as a Religious Society.* The Church Power *they own and exercise, and that which they reject and condemn: With the* Method *of their Proceedings against erring and disorderly Persons.*

THIS People increasing daily both in Town and Country, an *holy Care* fell upon some of the *Elders* among them, for the Benefit and Service of the Church. And the first Business in their View, after the Example of the primitive Saints, was the *Exercise of Charity*; to supply the Necessities of the Poor, and answer the like Occasions. Wherefore *Collections* were early and liberally made for that and divers other Services in the Church, and intrusted with faithful Men, fearing God, and of good Report, who were not weary in Welldoing; adding often of *their own*, in large Proportions, which they never brought to Account, or desired should be known, much less restored to them, that none might want, or any Service be retarded or disappointed.

They were also very careful that every one that belonged to them answered their Profession in their *Behaviour* among Men, upon all Occasions; that they lived *peaceably*, and were in all Things *good Examples*. They found themselves engaged to record their *Sufferings and Services*: And in the Case of *Marriage*, which they could not perform

perform in the ufual Methods of the Nation, but among themfelves, they took Care that all Things were *clear* between the Parties and all others: And it was then rare, that any one entertain'd an Inclination to a Perfon on that Account, till he or fhe had communicated it fecretly to fome very weighty and eminent Friends among them, that they might have a Senfe of the Matter; looking to the Council and Unity of their Brethren as of great Moment to them. But becaufe the Charge of the Poor, the Number of Orphans, Marriages, Sufferings, and other Matters, *multiplied*; and that it was good that the Churches were in fome Way and Method of proceeding in fuch Affairs among them, to the End they might the better correfpond upon Occafion, where a Member of one Meeting might have to do with one of another; it pleafed the Lord in his Wifdom and Goodnefs, to open the Underftanding of the *firft Inftrument* of this *Difpenfation* of *Life*, about a good and orderly Way of proceeding; who felt an holy Concern to vifit the Churches in Perfon throughout this Nation, to begin and eftablifh it among them: And by *his Epiftles*, the like was done in other Nations and Provinces abroad; which he alfo afterwards vifited, and helped in that Service, which fhall be obferved when I come to fpeak of him.

Now the *Care, Conduct* and *Difcipline*, I have been fpeaking of, and which are now practifed among this People, is as followeth.

This *Godly Elder*, in every County where he travelled, exhorted them, that *fome out of every* Meeting of Worfhip, fhould meet together once

in

in the Month, to confer about the Wants and Occasions of the Church. And as the Case required, so those *Monthly Meetings* were fewer or more in Number in every respective County: Four or Six Meetings of Worship, usually making one *Monthly Meeting* of *Business*. And accordingly the Brethren met him from Place to Place, and began the said Meetings, *viz.* For the *Poor*, *Orphans*, *orderly Walking*, *Integrity* to their *Profession*, *Births*, *Marriages*, *Burials*, *Sufferings*, &c. And that these *Monthly Meetings* should, in each County, make up *one Quarterly Meeting*, where the most zealous and eminent Friends of the County should *Assemble* to *communicate*, *advise* and *help one another*, especially when any Business seemed difficult, or a *Monthly Meeting* was tender of determining a Matter.

Also that these several *Quarterly Meetings* should digest the Reports of their *Monthly Meetings*, and prepare One for each respective *County*, against the *Yearly Meeting*, in which all *Quarterly Meetings* resolve; which is held in *London*: Where the Churches in this Nation, and other Nations, and Provinces, meet by *chosen Members* of their respective Counties, both *mutually* to communicate their *Church-Affairs*, and to advise, and be advised, in any depending Case to Edification. Also to provide a *requisite Stock* for the Discharge of general Expences for general Services in the Church, not needful to be here particularized.

At these Meetings any of the Members of the Churches may come, if they please, and speak their Minds freely, in the Fear of God, to any Matter; but the Mind of each *Quarterly Meeting*, therein

therein reprefented, is chiefly underftood, as to particular Cafes, in the Senfe delivered by the Perfons deputed, or chofen for that Service by the faid Meeting.

During their *Yearly Meeting*, to which their other Meetings refer in their Order, and naturally refolve themfelves, Care is taken by a *felect Number* for that Service, chofen by the general Affembly, to draw up the *Minutes* of the faid Meeting, upon the feveral Matters that have been under Confideration therein, to the End that the refpective *Quarterly* and *Monthly Meetings* may be informed of all Proceedings; together with a general Exhortation to *Holinefs, Unity* and *Charity*. Of all which Proceedings in the *Yearly, Monthly* and *Quarterly Meetings*, due Record is kept by fome One appointed for that Service, or that hath voluntarily undertaken it. Thefe Meetings are opened, and ufually concluded in their folemn Waiting upon God, who is fometimes gracioufly pleafed to anfwer them with *as fignal* Evidences of His Love and Prefence, as in any of their Meetings of Worfhip.

It is further to be noted, that in thefe *folemn Affemblies*, for the Churches Service, there is no One prefides among them after the Manner of the Affemblies of other People; Chrift only being their *Prefident*, as He is pleafed to appear in Life and Wifdom in any One or more of them, to whom, whatever be their Capacity or Degree, the reft adhere with a firm Unity, not of Authority but *Conviction*, which is the divine Authority and Way of Chrift's Power and Spirit in His People: Making good his blefled Promife, *That He would*

would be in the Midst of His, where and whenever they were met together in His Name, even to the End of the World. So be it.

Now it may be expected, I should here set down what Sort of *Authority* is exercised by this People, upon such Members of their Society as correspond not in their *Lives* with their *Profession*, and that are *Refractory* to this good and wholesome Order settled among them; and the rather, because they have not wanted their Reproach and Sufferings from some Tongues and Pens, upon this Occasion, in a plentiful Manner.

The Power they exercise, is such as Christ has given to His own People, to the End of the World, in the Persons of His Disciples, *viz.* To *oversee, exhort, reprove*, and after *long suffering* and *waiting* upon the *Disobedient* and *Refractory*, to *disown them*, as any more of their *Communion*, or that they will any longer stand charged in the Sight and Judgment of God or Men, with *their Conversation or Behaviour* as any *of them*, until they *repent*. The subject Matter about which this Authority, in any of the foregoing Branches of it, is exercised, is *first*, in Relation to *common* and *general Practice*. And, *secondly*, about those Things that more strictly refer to their own Character and *Profession*, and which distinguish them from all other Professors of *Christianity*; avoiding two Extreams upon which many split, viz. *Persecution* and *Libertinism*, that is, a Coercive Power, to *whip People into the Temple*; that such as will not conform, though against Faith and Conscience, shall be punish'd in their *Persons* or *Estates*: Or leaving all loose and at large, as to *Practice*; and so unaccountable

countable to all but God and the Magistrate. To which hurtful Extream, nothing has more contributed than the Abuse of *Church Power*, by such as suffer their Passions and private Interests to prevail with them to carry it to outward Force and Corporal Punishment. A Practice they have been taught to dislike, by their extream Sufferings, as well as their known Principle for an *universal Liberty* of *Conscience*.

On the other Hand, they equally dislike an *Independency* in Society; an *Unaccountableness* in *Practice* and *Conversation* to the *Rules* and *Terms* of their own Communion, and to those that are the Members of it. They distinguish between imposing any Practice that immediately regards *Faith* or *Worship*, (which is never to be done or suffered, or submitted unto) and requiring *Christian* Compliance with those Methods that only respect Church-Business in its more *Civil* Part and Concern; and that regard the *discreet* and *orderly Maintenance* of the Character of the Society as a *sober* and *religious Community*. In short, what is for the Promotion of *Holiness* and *Charity*, that Men may practise what they profess, live up to *their own Principles*, and not be at Liberty to give the *Lye* to their own Profession without Rebuke, is their *Use* and *Limit* of Church Power. They compel none *to join them*, but oblige those that are of them to walk *suitable*, or they are *denied* by them: That is all the *Mark* they set upon them, and the *Power* they exercise, or judge a *Christian* Society can exercise, upon those that are Members of it.

The Way of their Proceeding against such as have lapsed or transgressed, is this. He is visited by by some of them, and the Matter of Fact is laid home to him, be it any evil Practice against known and general Virtue, or any Branch of their particular Testimony, which he, in common, professeth with them. They labour with him in much Love and Zeal, for the *Good* of his Soul, the Honour of God, and *Reputation* of their Profession, to *own* his Fault and condemn it, in as ample a Manner as the Evil or Scandal was given by him; which for the most Part is perform'd by some *written* Testimony under the Party's Hand: And if it so happen, that the Party prove *Refractory*, and is not willing to clear the Truth, they profess, from the Reproach of his or her evil Doing or Unfaithfulness, they, after repeated Entreaties and due waiting for a Token of Repentance, give forth a Paper to disown such a Fact, and the Party offending: *Recording* the same as a Testimony of their Care for the Honour of the Truth they profess.

And if he or she shall clear their *Profession* and themselves, by sincere Acknowledgment of their Fault, and Godly Sorrow for so doing, they are *received* and *looked upon again as Members of their Communion*. For as God, so his true People, *upbraid no Man* after Repentance.

This is the Account I had to give of the People of God called *Quakers*, as to their *Rise*, *Appearance*, *Principles* and *Practices* in this Age of the World, both with Respect to their *Faith* and *Worship*, *Discipline* and *Conversation*. And I judge it very proper in this Place, because it is to *preface* the *Journal* of the *first* blessed and glorious Instrument of this Work, and for a Testimony
to

to him in his singular *Qualifications* and *Services*, in which he *abundantly excelled* in this Day, and are worthy to be set forth as an *Example* to all *succeeding Times*, to the Glory of the *Most High* God, and for a *just Memorial* to that *worthy* and *excellent Man*, his *faithful Servant* and *Apostle* to this Generation of the World.

CHAP. V.

Of the first Instrument *or* Person *by whom God was pleased to gather this People into the Way they profess.* His Name GEORGE FOX: *His many excellent Qualifications; shewing a* divine, *and not an* human Power *to have been their* Original *in him.* His Troubles *and* Sufferings *both from without and within.* His End *and* Triumph.

I Am now come to the third Head or Branch of my *Preface*, viz. The *instrumental* Author. For it is natural for some to say, Well, here is the People and Work, but where and who was the *Man*, the *Instrument?* He that in this Age was sent to begin this Work and People? I shall, as God shall enable me, declare who and what he was; not only by Report of others, but from my own long and most inward Converse, and intimate Knowledge of him; for which my Soul *blesseth* God, as it hath often done: And I doubt not, but by that Time I have discharged myself of this Part of my *Preface*, my serious Readers will believe I had good Cause so to do.

The blessed Instrument of, and in this Day of God, and of whom I am now about to write, was

GEORGE

George Fox, diftinguifhed from another of that Name, by that other's Addition of *younger* to his Name, in all his Writings; not that he was fo in Years; but that he was fo in the Truth: But he was alfo a worthy Man, Witnefs and Servant of God in his Time.

But this George Fox was born in *Leicefterfhire*, about the Year 1624. He defcended of honeft and fufficient Parents, who endeavoured to bring him up, as they did the Reft of their Children, in the Way and Worfhip of the *Nation*: Efpecially his Mother, who was a Woman accomplifhed above moft of her Degree in the Place where fhe lived. But from a Child he appeared of *another Frame* of Mind than the Reft of his Brethren; being *more religious, inward, ftill, folid,* and *obferving beyond his Years*, as the Anfwers he would give, and the Queftions he would put, upon Occafion, manifefted, to the Aftonifhment of thofe that heard him, efpecially in *divine Things*.

His Mother taking Notice of his *fingular Temper*, and the *Gravity, Wifdom* and *Piety*, that very early fhined thro' him, refufing *Childifh* and *vain Sports* and *Company*, when very young: She was tender and indulgent over him, fo that from her he met with little Difficulty. As to his *Employment*, he was brought up in Country Bufinefs, and as he took moft Delight in *Sheep*, fo he was very fkilful in them; an Employment that very well fuited his Mind in feveral Refpects, both for its *Innocency* and *Solitude*; and was a *juft Emblem* of his after *Miniftry* and *Service*.

I fhall not break in upon his own Account, which is by much the beft that can be given, and therefore

therefore defire, what I can to avoid faying any Thing of what is faid already, as to the particular Paffages of his coming forth: But, in general, when he was fomewhat above Twenty, he left his Friends, and vifited the moft *retired* and *religious* People in thofe Parts: And fome there were, in this Nation, *who waited for the Confolation of* Ifrael, *Night and Day,* as *Zacharias, Anna,* and good old *Simeon* did of old Time. To thefe he was fent, and thefe he fought out in the neighbouring Counties, and among them he fojourned, till his more ample Miniftry came upon him. At this Time he taught, and was an Example of *Silence,* endeavouring to bring them from Self-performances: Teftifying of, and turning them to the *Light of* Chrift *within them,* and encouraging them to wait in *Patience,* and to feel the Power of it to ftir in their Hearts, that their Knowledge and Worfhip of God might ftand in the Power of an *endlefs* Life, which was to be found in the *Light* as it was obeyed in the Manifeftation of it in Man. *For in the Word was Life, and that Life is the Light of Men. Life* in the Word, *Light* in Men, and *Life* in Men too, as the *Light* is obey'd: The Children of the Light living by the Life of the Word, by which the Word begets them again to God, which is the *Regeneration* and *New Birth,* without which there is no coming into the Kingdom of God: And to which whoever comes, is *greater* than *John;* that is, than *John's* Difpenfation, which was not that of the Kingdom, but the Confummation of the Legal, and Fore-running of the *Gofpel-Times,* the Time of the *Kingdom.* Accordingly feveral

Meetings were gather'd in those Parts; and thus his Time was employ'd for some Years.

In 1652, he being in his usual Retirement, his Mind exercised towards the Lord, upon a very high Mountain, in some of the hither Parts of *Yorkshire*, as I take it, he had a *Vision* of the *great Work* of God in the Earth, and of the Way that he was to go forth in a *publick Ministry*, to begin it. He saw People as thick as *Motes* in the *Sun*, that should in Time be brought home to the Lord, that there might be but one Shepherd and one Sheepfold in all the Earth. There his Eye was directed *Northward*, beholding a great People that should receive him and his Message in those Parts. Upon this Mountain he was mov'd of the Lord to sound out His *great* and *notable Day*, as if he had been in a great Auditory; and from thence went *North*, as the Lord had shewn him. And in every Place where he came, if not before he came to it, he had his particular Exercise and Service *shewn* to him, so that the Lord was his *Leader* indeed. For it was not in vain that he travelled; God in most Places *sealing* his Commission with the *Convincement* of some of all Sorts, as well Publicans as sober Professors of Religion. Some of the first and most eminent of those that came forth in a publick Ministry, and which are now at Rest, were *Richard Farnsworth, James Naylor, William Dewsberry, Thomas Aldam, Francis Howgil, Edward Burroughs, John Camm, John Audland, Richard Hubberthorn, T. Taylor, T. Holmes, Alexander Parker, William Simson, William Caton, John Stubbs, Robert Withers, Thomas Loe, Josiah Coale, John Burnyeat, Robert Lodge, Thomas*

Thomas Salthouse, and many more Worthies, that cannot be well here nam'd ; together with divers *yet living* of the first and great Convincement, who, after the *Knowledge of God's purging Judgment in themselves, and sometime of waiting in Silence* upon Him, to *feel* and *receive Power from on high*, to speak in His Name, (which none else rightly can, though they may use the same Words) They felt its divine Motions, and were frequently drawn forth, especially to visit the *publick Assemblies*, to reprove, inform, and exhort them: Sometimes in *Markets*, *Fairs*, *Streets*, and by the *Highway-side*, calling People to Repentance, and to turn to the Lord with their Hearts as well as their Mouths; directing them to the Light of Christ *within* them, to see, examine, and consider their Ways by, and to *eschew Evil,* and *do the good and acceptable Will of* God. And they suffered great Hardships for this their Love and Good-will; being *often stockt, stoned, beaten, whipt* and *imprisoned*; though honest Men, and of good Report where they liv'd; that had left Wives, Children, and Houses, and Lands, to visit them with a *living Call* to Repentance. And though the *Priests* generally set themselves to oppose them, and writ against them, and insinuated most false and scandalous Stories to defame them; stirring up the Magistrates to suppress them, especially in those *Northeren* Parts; yet God was pleased so to fill them with His living Power, and give them such an open Door of Utterance in His Service, that there was a mighty Convincement over those Parts.

And through the tender and singular Indulgence of Judge *Bradshaw* and Judge *Fell*, and Colonel

lonel *West*, in the Infancy of Things, the *Priests* were never able to gain the Point they laboured for, which was to have proceeded to *Blood*; and, if possible, *Herod* like, by a cruel Exercise of the Civil Power, to have cut them off, and rooted them out of the Country. But especially Judge *Fell*, who was not only a Check to their Rage in the Course of legal Proceedings, but otherwise, upon Occasion; and finally countenanced this People. For his Wife receiving the Truth with the first, it had that Influence upon his Spirit, being a *just* and *wise* Man, and seeing in his own Wife and Family a full Confutation of all the popular Clamours against the Way of *Truth*, that he covered them what he could, and freely opened his Doors, and gave up his House to his Wife and her Friends: not valuing the Reproach of ignorant or Evil-minded People; which I here mention to his and her Honour, and which will be, I believe an *Honour* and a *Blessing* to such of their Name and Family, as shall be found in that *Tenderness*, *Humility*, *Love* and *Zeal* for the *Truth* and *People* of the Lord.

That House was for some Years, at first especially, 'till the *Truth* had opened its Way into the *Southern* Parts of this Island, an eminent Receptacle of this People. Others, of good Note and Substance in those *Northern* Countries, had also opened their Houses, together with their Hearts, to the many *Publishers*, that, in a short Time, the Lord had raised to declare his Salvation to the People; and where Meetings of the Lord's *Messengers* were frequently held, to communicate their

Services

Services and *Exercises*, and comfort and edify one another in their *blessed Ministry*.

But lest this may be thought a *Digression*, having touch'd upon this before, I return to this *excellent* Man : And for his Personal Qualities, both *natural, moral* and *divine*, as they appeared in his Converse with the Brethren ; and in the Church of God, take as follows :

I. He was a Man that God endued with a *clear* and *wonderful* Depth : A *Discerner* of other's Spirits, and very much a *Master* of his own. And tho' that Side of his Understanding which lay next to the World, and especially the Expression of it, might sound *uncouth* and *unfashionable* to nice Ears, his Matter was nevertheless very profound ; and would not only bear to be often consider'd, but the more it was so, the more weighty and instructing it appear'd. And as *abruptly* and *brokenly* as sometimes his Sentences would seem to fall from him, about *divine Things*, it is well known they were often as *Texts* to many fairer Declarations. And indeed, it shewed, beyond all Contradiction, that God *sent him* ; in that *no Art* or *Parts* had any *Share* in the *Matter* or *Manner* of his *Ministry* ; and that so many *great, excellent,* and *necessary Truths* as he came forth to preach to Mankind, had therefore nothing of Man's Wit or Wisdom to recommend them. So that as to Man he was an *Original*, being *no Man*'s Copy. And his Ministry and Writings shew they are from one that was not taught of Man, nor had learned what he said by Study. Nor were they notional or speculative, but *sensible* and *practical Truths*, tending to *Conversion* and *Regeneration*, and the setting up of the Kingdom of

E   God

God *in the Hearts of* Men : And the Way of it was his Work. So that I have many Times been overcome in myself, and been made to say, with my Lord and Master, upon the like Occasion, *I thank thee, O Father, Lord of Heaven and Earth, that Thou hast hid these Things from the Wise and Prudent of this World, and revealed them to Babes:* For many Times hath my Soul *bowed* in an *humble Thankfulness* to the Lord, that He did not choose any of the Wise and Learned of this World to be the *first* Messenger in our Age, of *His blessed Truth* to Men ; but that He took one that was not of *high Degree*, or *elegant Speech*, or *learned* after the Way of this World, that, His Message and Work, He sent him to do, might come with *less Suspicion*, or Jealousy of human Wisdom and Interest, and with *more Force and Clearness upon the Consciences* of those that sincerely sought the Way of *Truth* in the Love of it. I say, beholding with the Eye of my Mind, which the God of Heaven had opened in me, the *Marks* of God's Finger and Hand *visibly* in this Testimony, from the *Clearness* of the Principle, the Power and Efficacy of it, in the *exemplary* Sobriety, Plainness, Zeal, Steadiness, Humility, Gravity, Punctuality, Charity, and *circumspect* Care in the Government of Church-Affairs, which shined in his and their Life and Testimony that God employ'd in this Work, it greatly *confirmed me that it was of* God, and engaged my Soul in a *deep Love, Fear, Reverence* and *Thankfulness* for His *Love* and *Mercy* therein to Mankind: In which Mind I remain, and shall, I hope, through the Lord's Strength, to the End of my Days.

II. In his *Testimony* or *Ministry*, he much laboured

ed to open Truth to the People's Understandings, and to *bottom* them upon the *Principle* and *Principal*, Christ Jesus the *Light* of the *World*; that by bringing them to something that was from God in themselves, they might the better know and judge of Him and themselves.

III. He had an extraordinary Gift in *Opening* the Scriptures. He would go to the *Marrow* of Things, and shew the *Mind, Harmony* and *fulfiling* of them with much Plainness, and to great Comfort and Edification.

IV. The Mystery of the *first* and *second Adam*, of the *Fall* and *Restoration*, of the *Law* and *Gospel*, of *Shadows* and *Substance*, of the *Servant's* and *Son's State*, and the fulfilling of the Scriptures in Christ and by Christ the *true Light*, in all that are His, through the Obedience of *Faith*, were much of the *Substance* and *Drift* of his Testimonies. In all which he was witnessed to be of God; being sensibly felt to speak that which he had received of Christ, and was his own Experience, in that which never errs nor fails.

V. But above all, he excelled in *Prayer*. The *Inwardness* and *Weight* of his Spirit, the *Reverence* and *Solemnity* of his Address and Behaviour, and the *Fewness* and *Fulness* of his Words, have often struck even *Strangers* with *Admiration*, as they used to reach others with *Consolation*. The most *awful, living, reverent Frame*, I ever felt or beheld, I must say, was his in *Prayer*. And truly it was a Testimony he knew and lived nearer to the Lord than other Men; for they that know Him most, will see most Reason to approach Him with *Reverence* and *Fear*.

VI. He was of an *innocent Life*, no *Busy-body*, nor *Self-seeker*; neither *touchy* nor *critical*: What fell from him was very *inoffensive*, if not very edifying. So *meek, contented, modest, easy, steady, tender*; it was a Pleasure to be in his Company. He exercised no Authority but over Evil, and that every where, and in all; but with *Love, Compassion,* and *Long-suffering*. A most merciful Man, as ready to forgive, as unapt to take or give an Offence. Thousands can truly say he was of an *excellent Spirit* and *Savour* among them, and because thereof, the most excellent Spirits loved him with an *unfeigned* and *unfading Love*.

VII. He was an *incessant Labourer*: For in his younger Time, before his many, great and deep Sufferings and Travels had enfeebled his Body for Itinerant Services, he *laboured much* in the *Word* and *Doctrine*, and *Discipline*, in *England, Scotland,* and *Ireland*; *turning* many to God, and *confirming* those that were convinced of the *Truth*, and *settling good Order*, as to Church Affairs, among them. And towards the Conclusion of his travelling Service, between the Years *Seventy-one* and *Seventy-seven*, he visited the Churches of Christ in the Plantations in *America*, and in the *united Provinces*, and *Germany*, as his Journal relates; to the Convincement and Consolation of many. After that Time he chiefly resided in and about the *City* of *London*: And besides his Labour in the Ministry, which was frequent and servicable, he *writ much*, both to them that are within, and those that are without the Communion. But the Care he took of the Affairs of the Church in general was very great.

VIII.

VIII. He was often where the *Records* of the Business of the Church are kept, and where the Letters from the many Meetings of God's People over all the World use to come: Which Letters he had read to him, and communicated them to the Meeting, that is weekly held, for such Services; and he would be sure to stir them up to answer them, especially in suffering Cases: Showing great *Sympathy*, and Compassion upon all such Occasions; carefully looking into the respective Cases, and endeavouring speedy Relief, according to the Nature of them. So that the Churches, or any of the suffering Members thereof, were sure not to be forgotten or delayed in their Desires, if he was there.

IX. As he was unwearied, so he was *undaunted* in his Services for God and his People; he was no more to be moved to *Fear* than to *Wrath*. His Behaviour at *Derby*, *Litchfield*, *Appleby*, before *Oliver Cromwell*, *Launceston*, *Scarborough*, *Worcester*, and *Westminster-Hall*, with many other Places and Exercises, did abundantly evidence it, to his Enemies as well as his Friends.

But as, in the primitive Times, some rose up against the *blessed Apostles* of our Lord Jesus Christ, even from among those that they had turned to the Hope of the Gospel, and they became their greatest trouble; so this Man of God had *his Share* of Suffering from some that were convinced *by him*, who, thro' Prejudice or Mistake, ran against him, as one that sought Dominion over Conscience, because he prest, by his Presence or Epistles, a ready and zealous Compliance with such good and wholesome Things as tended to an

orderly

orderly Conversation about the Affairs of the Church, and in their walking before Men. That which contributed much to this ill Work was, in some, a *begrudging* of this meek Man the Love and Esteem he had and deserved in the Hearts of the People, and *Weakness* in others, that were taken with their groundless Suggestions of *Imposition* and *blind Obedience*.

They would have had every Man *independent*, that as he had the Principle in himself, he should only stand and fall to that, and no Body else: Not considering that the Principle is *one* in all; and though the Measure of Light or Grace might *differ*, yet the Nature of it was the *same*; and being so, they struck at the *Spiritual Unity*, which a People, guided by the same Principle, are naturally led into: So that what is an Evil to *one*, is so to *all*, and what is virtuous, honest, and of good Repute to *one*, is so to *all*, from the Sense and Savour of the *one universal Principle* which is common to all, and which the *Disaffected* also profess to be the Root of all true *Christian* Fellowship, and that Spirit into which the People of God *drink*, and come to be Spiritually-minded, and of *one Heart* and *one Soul*.

Some weakly mistook *good Order* in the Government of Church-Affairs, for *Discipline* in *Worship*, and that it was so prest or recommended by him and other Brethren. And thereupon they were ready to reflect the same Things that *Dissenters* had very reasonably objected upon the *National Churches*, that have coercively pressed *Conformity* to their respective *Creeds* and *Worships*. Whereas these Things related *wholly to Conversation*, and the *Outward* (and as I may say) *Civil Part* of the

the *Church*; that Men should walk up to the Principles of their Belief, and not be wanting in Care and Charity. But though some have stumbled and fallen through Mistakes, and an unreasonable Obstinacy even to a Prejudice; yet blessed be God, the Generality have returned to their *first Love*, and seen the Work of the Enemy, that loses no Opportunity or Advantage by which he may check or hinder the Work of God, and disquiet the Peace of his Church, and chill the Love of His People to the Truth, and one to another; and there is Hope of divers of the few that yet are at a Distance.

In all these Occasions, though there was no Person the *Discontented* struck so sharply at, as this good *Man*, he bore all their Weakness and Prejudice, and returned not Reflection for Reflection; but forgave them their weak and bitter Speeches, praying for them, that they might have a Sense of their Hurt, and see the Subtilty of the Enemy to rend and divide, and return into their first Love that thought no Ill.

And truly I must say, that though God had visibly clothed him with a *divine Preference* and *Authority*, and indeed his very Presence exprest a *religious Majesty*; yet he never abused it; but held his Place in the Church of God with *great Meekness*, and a most *engaging Humility* and *Moderation*. For upon all Occasions, like his blessed Master, he was a *Servant to all*; holding and exercising his Eldership in the invisible Power that had gathered them, with Reverence to the Head and Care over the Body: And was received, only in that Spirit and Power of Christ, as the *first* and *chief Elder* in this Age: Who, as he was therefore worthy of double Honour, so for the same Reason it was given by the *Faithful* of this Day; because his Authority was inward and not outward, and that he got it and kept it by the Love of God, and Power of an endless Life. I write my Knowledge, and not Report, and *my Witness is true*; having been with him for Weeks and Months together on divers Occasions, and those of the nearest and most exercising Nature; and that by Night and by Day, by Sea and by Land; in this and in foreign Countries: And I can say, I never saw him *out of his Place*, or not a Match for every Service or Occasion.

For in all Things he acquitted himself like *a Man*, yea, *a strong Man*, a *new* and *Heavenly-minded* Man, a *Divine* and a *Naturalist*, and all of God Almighty's making. I have been surprised at his Questions and Answers in *natural* Things: That whilst he was ignorant of useless and Sophistical Science, he had in him the Grounds of useful and commendable Knowledge, and cherished it every where. Civil, *beyond all Forms of Breeding*, in his Behaviour: Very Temperate, Eating little, and Sleeping less, though a bulky Person.

Thus he lived and sojourned among us: And as he lived so he died; feeling the same eternal Power, that had raised and preserved him, in his last Moments. So full of *Assurance* was he, that he triumph'd over *Death*; and so even in his Spirit to the last, as if Death were hardly worth Notice, or a Mention: Recommending to some of us with him, the Dispatch and Dispersion of

an

an *Epistle* just before given forth by him to the Churches of Christ throughout the World, and his own Books: But above all, *Friends*; and of all *Friends*, those in *Ireland* and *America*, twice over, saying, *Mind Poor Friends in* Ireland *and* America.

And to some that came in and enquired how he found himself, he answered, *Never heed, the* Lord's *Power is over all* Weakness *and* Death; *the Seed* reigns, *blessed be the* Lord: Which was about four or five Hours before his Departure out of this World. He was at the great Meeting near *Lombard-street*, on the First Day of the Week, and it was the third following about Ten at Night when he left us; being at the House of *Henry Goldney* in the same Court. In a good old Age he went, after, having lived to see *his Children's Children* in the *Truth* to *many Generations*. He had the Comfort of a short Illness, and the Blessing of a clear Sense to the last: And we may truly say, with a Man of God of old, *That being dead, he yet speaketh*; And though now absent in Body, *he is present in Spirit*: Neither Time nor Place being able to interrupt the Communion of Saints, or dissolve the Fellowship of the Spirits of the Just. His Works praise him, because they are to the Praise of Him that wrought by him; for which his Memorial is and shall be blessed. I have done, as to this Part of my *Preface*, when I have left this short Epitaph to his Name, *Many Sons have done virtuously in this Day*; *but dear* GEORGE, *thou excellest them all*.

CHAP.

CHAP. VI.

Containing five several Exhortations. *First,* general, *reminding this People of their* primitive Integrity *and* Simplicity. *Secondly,* in particular, *to the* Ministry. *Thirdly, to the* Young Convinced. *Fourthly, to the* Children *of* Friends. *Fifthly, to those that are yet* Strangers *to this* People *and* Way, *to whom this Book, (and that it was* Preface *to in its former Edition) may come. All the several* Exhortations *accommodated to their several* States *and* Conditions; *that all may answer the End of* God's Glory, *and their own Salvation.*

AND now, *Friends,* you that profess to walk in the Way that this blessed Man was sent of God to turn us into, suffer, I beseech you, the Word of Exhortation, as well *Fathers* as *Children,* and *Elders* as *young Men.* The *Glory* of this Day, and *Foundation* of the Hope that has not made us ashamed since we were a People, you know, is that blessed Principle of Light and Life of Christ which we profess, and direct all People to, as the *great* and *divine Instrument* and *Agent* of Man's Conversion to God. It was by this that we were first touched, and effectually enlightened, as to our inward State; which put us upon the Consideration of our latter End, causing us to set the Lord before our Eyes, and to number our Days, that we might apply our Hearts to Wisdom. In that Day we judged not after the *Sight* of the *Eye,*

Of the People called QUAKERS. 67

or after the *Hearing* of the *Ear*, but according to the *Light* and *Sense* this *blessed Principle* gave us, so we judged and acted in Reference to Things and Persons, ourselves and others; yea, towards God our Maker. For being quick'ned by it in our *inward Man*, we could easily discern the Difference of Things, and feel what was right, and what was wrong, and what was fit, and what not, both in Reference to *Religious* and *Civil Concerns*. That being the Ground of the Fellowship of all Saints, it was in that our Fellowship stood. In this we desired to have a Sense of one another, acted towards one another, and all Men; in *Love*, *Faithfulness* and *Fear*.

In feeling of the *Stirrings* and *Motions* of this Principle in our Hearts, we drew near to the Lord, and waited to be prepared by it, that we might *feel Drawings* and *Movings* before we *approached* the Lord in Prayer, or open'd our Mouths in *Ministry*. And in our Beginning and Ending with *this* stood our *Comfort, Service* and *Edification*. And as we ran faster or fell short, in our *Services*, we made Burthens for ourselves to bear; finding in ourselves a Rebuke instead of an Acceptance; and in Lieu of well-done, *Who has required this at your Hands?* In that Day we were an exercised People, our very Countenances and Deportment declared it.

Care for others was then much upon us, as well as for ourselves; especially of the *young Convinced*. Often had we the Burthen of the Word of the Lord to our *Neighbours*, *Relations* and *Acquaintance*; and sometimes *Strangers* also. We were in Travail likewise for one another's Preservation; not seeking,

ing, but shuning Occasions of any Coldness or Misunderstanding: Treating one another as those that believed and felt God *present*: Which kept our Conversation *innocent*, *serious* and *weighty*; guarding ourselves against the Cares and Friendships of the World.

We held the Truth in the Spirit of it, and not in our own Spirits, or after our own Wills and Affections: They were bowed and brought into *subjection*, insomuch that it was visible to them that knew us; we did not think ourselves at our own *Disposal*, to go where we list, or say or do what we list or when we list. Our Liberty stood in the Liberty of the Spirit of Truth; and no Pleasure, no Profit, no Fear, no Favour could draw us from this retired, strict and watchful Frame. We were so far from seeking Occasions of Company, that we avoided them what we could; pursuing our own Business, with Moderation, instead of meddling with other People's *Unnecessarily*.

Our Words were few and Savoury, our Looks composed and weighty, and our whole Deportment very observable. True it is, that this retired and strict Sort of Life from the Liberty of the Conversation of the World, exposed us to the Censures of many as *Humourists*, *conceited* and *Self-righteous* Persons, &c. But it was our Preservation from many Snares, to which others were continually exposed, by the Prevalency of the Lust of the Eye, the Lust of the Flesh, and the Pride of Life, that wanted no Occasions or Temptations to excite them abroad in the Converse of the World.

I can-

I cannot forget the *Humility* and *chaste Zeal* of that Day. O, how *constant* at Meetings, how *retired* in them, how *firm* to *Truth's Life*, as well as *Truth's Principles!* And how *entire* and *united* in our Communion, as indeed became those that profess one Head even Christ Jesus the Lord.

This being the Testimony and Example the Man of God, before-mentioned, was sent to declare and leave amongst us, and we having embraced the same, as the *merciful Visitation* of God to us, the Word of Exhortation at this Time is, *That we continue to be found in the Way of this Testimony, with all Zeal and Integrity, and so much the more, by how much the Day draweth near.*

And *first*, as to you my *beloved* and much *honored Brethren* in Christ, that are in the Exercise of the *Ministry*: O, feel *Life* in your *Ministry!* Let *Life* be your Commission, your Well-spring and Treasury on all such Occasions; else, you well know, there can be no *begetting* to God, since nothing can quicken or make people alive to God, but the Life of God: And it must be a Ministry *in* and *from Life*, that enlivens any People to God. We have seen the Fruit of all other Ministries, by the few that are *turned* from the Evil of their Ways. It is not our *Parts*, or *Memory*, or the *Repetition* of *former Openings*, in our own Will and Time, that will do God's Work. A dry Doctrinal Ministry, however sound in Words, can reach but the Ear, and is but a *Dream* at the best: There is another Soundness, that is soundest of all, *viz.* Christ *the Power of* God. This is the Key of *David, that opens and none shuts, and shuts, and none can open:* As the Oil to the Lamp, and the Soul to the

the Body, so is that to the best of Words. Which made Christ to say, *My Words, they are* Spirit, *and they are* Life; that is, they are from Life, and therefore they make you alive, that receive them. If the Disciples, that had lived with Jesus, were to stay at *Jerusalem*, till they received it; much more must we *wait to receive* before we *minister*, if we will turn People from Darkness to Light, and from Satan's Power to God.

I fervently bow my Knees to the God and Father of our Lord Jesus Christ, that you may always be like minded, that you may *ever wait reverently*, for the Coming and Opening of the Word of Life, and attend upon it in your Ministry and Service, that you may serve God in His Spirit. And be it little or be it much, it is well; for much is not too much, and the least is enough, if from the Motion of God's Spirit; and without it, verily, never so little is too much, because to no Profit.

For it is the Spirit of the Lord *immediately* or *through the Ministry* of His Servants, that teacheth His People to profit; and to be sure, so far as we take Him along with us in our Services, so far we are profitable and no farther. For if it be the Lord that must work all Things in us for our *Salvation*, much more is it the Lord that must work in us for the *Conversion* of others. If therefore it was once a Cross to us *to speak*, though the Lord required it at our Hands; let it never be so to be *silent*, when he does not.

It is one of the most dreadful Sayings in the Book of God, *That he that adds to the Words of the Prophecy of this Book,* God *will add to him the Plagues*

Plagues written in this Book. To keep *back* the Counsel of God, is as terrible; *for he that takes away from the Words of the Book of this Prophecy*, God *shall take away his Part out of the Book of Life.* And truly, it has great *Caution* in it, to those that use the Name of the Lord, to be well assured the Lord *speaks*, that they may not be found of the Number of those that add to the Words of the Testimony of Prophecy, which the Lord giveth them to bear; nor yet to mince or diminish the same, both being so very offensive to God.

Wherefore, *Brethren*, let us be careful neither to *out-go* our Guide, nor yet *loiter* behind him; since he that makes Haste, may miss his Way, and he that stays behind, lose his Guide. For even those that have received the Word of the Lord, had need *wait* for Wisdom, that they may see how to divide the Word *aright*: Which plainly implieth that it is possible for one, that hath received the Word of the Lord, to miss in the dividing and Application of it, which must come from an *Impatiency* of Spirit, and a Self-working, which makes an unsound and dangerous Mixture; and will hardly beget a right-minded living People to God.

I am earnest in this above all other Considerations, as to *publick Brethren*; well knowing how much it concerns the present and future State, and Preservation of the Church of Christ Jesus, that has been gathered and built up by a *living* and *powerful Ministry*, that the Ministry be held, preserved, and continued in the Manifestations, Motions and Supplies of the *same Life* and *Power*, from Time to Time.

And where-ever it is observed, that any do minister more from *Gifts*, and *Parts*, than *Life* and *Power*, tho' they have an enlightned and doctrinal Understanding, let them in Time be advised and admonished for their Preservation, because insensibly such will come to depend upon a *Self-sufficiency*; to forsake Christ the living Fountain, and hew out unto themselves *Cisterns* that will hold no *living Waters*: And by Degrees, such will come to draw others from *waiting* upon the Gift of God in themselves, and to feel it in others, in order to their *Strength* and *Refreshment*, to wait upon them, and to turn from God to Man again, and so make Shipwreck of the Faith once delivered to the Saints, and of a good Conscience towards God; which are only kept by that divine Gift of Life, that begat the one, and awaken'd and sanctified the other in the Beginning.

Nor is it enough, that we have *known* the divine Gift, and in it have reached to the *Spirits in Prison*, and been the Instruments of the Convincing of others of the Way of God, if we keep not as low and poor in ourselves, and as depending upon the Lord as ever: Since no *Memory*, no *Repetitions* of *former Openings, Revelations* or *Enjoyments*, will bring a Soul to God, or afford *Bread* to the Hungry, or *Water* to the Thirsty, unless Life go with what we say, and that must be *waited for*.

O that we may have *no other Fountain, Treasure* or *Dependence!* That none may presume at any Rate to act of themselves for God, because they have long acted from God; that we may not supply Want of waiting with our own Wisdom, or think that we may take less Care and more Liberty

in

in speaking than formerly; and that where we do not feel the Lord by *His Power*, to open us and enlarge us, whatever be the Expectation of the People, or has been our customary Supply and Character, we may not exceed or fill up the Time with our own.

I hope we shall ever remember, who it was that said, *Of yourselves you can do nothing*: Our Sufficiency is in Him. And if we are not to speak our own *Words*, or *take Thought* what we should say to Men in our Defence, when exposed for our Testimony, surely we ought to speak none of our *own Words*, or *take Thought* what we shall say in our Testimony and Ministry, in the Name of our Lord, to the Souls of the People; for then of all Times, and of all other Occasions, should it be fulfilled in us, *for it is not you that* speak, *but the Spirit of my Father that* speaketh *in you*.

And indeed, the *Ministry* of the *Spirit* must, and does keep its *Analogy* and *Agreement* with the *Birth* of the *Spirit*, that as no Man can inherit the Kingdom of God, *unless he be born of the Spirit*, so no Ministry can beget a Soul to God, but that which is *from the Spirit*. For this, as I said before, the Disciples waited before they went forth; and in this, *our Elder Brethren*, and Messengers of God in our Day, *waited, visited,* and *reached to us*; and having begun in the *Spirit*, let none ever hope or seek to be made *perfect in the Flesh*: For what is the *Flesh* to the *Spirit*, or the *Chaff* to the *Wheat*? And if we keep in the Spirit, we shall keep in the *Unity* of it, which is the Ground of *true Fellowship*. For by *drinking* into that *one Spirit*, we are made one People to God, and

by

by it we are continued in the Unity of the Faith, and the Bond of Peace. No *envying*, no *Bitterness*, no *Strife*, can have Place with us. We shall watch always for Good, and not for Evil, one over another, and rejoice exceedingly, and not begrudge at *one another's Increase* in the Riches of the Grace with which God replenisheth His faithful Servants.

And *Brethren*, as to you is committed the *Dispensation* of the *Oracles* of God, which give you frequent Opportunities, and great Place with the People among whom you travel, I beseech you that you would not think it sufficient, to declare the Word of Life, in their *Assemblies*; however edifying and comfortable such Opportunities may be to you and them: But, as was the *Practice* of the Man of God before mentioned, in great Measure, when among us, inquire the *State* of the several Churches you visit; who among them are *afflicted* or *sick*, who are *tempted*, and if any are *unfaithful* or *obstinate*; and endeavour to issue those Things in the *Wisdom* and *Power* of God, which will be a glorious *Crown* upon *your Ministry*. As that prepares your Way in the Hearts of the People, to receive you as Men of God, so it gives you Credit with them to do them Good by your Advice in other Respects; the *Afflicted* will be comforted by you, the *Tempted* strengthened, the *Sick* refreshed, the *Unfaithful* convicted and restored, and such as are *obstinate*, softned and fitted for Reconciliation, which is clinching the Nail, and applying and fastning the general Testimony, by this *particular Care* of the several Branches of

it,

it, in Reference to them more immediately concerned in it.

For though *good* and *wife Men*, and *Elders too*, may reside in such Places, who are of Worth and Importance in the general, and in other Places; yet it does not always follow, that they may have the Room they deserve in the Hearts of the People they live among; or some particular Occasion may make it unfit for him or them to use that Authority. But you that travel as God's *Messengers*, if they receive you in the greater, shall they refuse you in the less? And if they own the general Testimony, can they withstand the *particular Application* of it, in their own Cases? Thus ye will shew yourselves Workmen indeed, and carry your Business before you, to the Praise of his Name, that hath called you from Darkness to Light, that you might turn others from Satan's *Power* unto God and his Kingdom, which is within. And O that there were more of such faithful *Labourers* in the *Vineyard* of the Lord! Never more Need since the Day of God.

Wherefore I cannot but cry and call aloud to you, that have been long *Professors* of the Truth, and know the Truth in the convincing Power of it, and have had a sober Conversation among Men, yet content yourselves only to know Truth for yourselves, to go to Meetings, and exercise an ordinary Charity in the Church, and an honest Behaviour in the World, and limit yourselves within those Bounds; feeling little or no Concern upon your Spirits for the Glory of the Lord in the Prosperity of His Truth in the Earth, more than to be glad that others succeed in such Service. *Arise ye* in the
Name

Name and *Power* of the Lord Jesus: Behold how white the Fields are unto Harvest, in this and other Nations, and how few able and faithful Labourers there are to work therein! Your Country-Folks, Neighbours and Kindred want to know the Lord and his Truth, and to walk in it. Does nothing lie at your Door upon their Account? Search and see, and lose no Time, I beseech you, for the Lord is at hand.

I do not judge you, there is one that judgeth all Men, and His Judgment is true. You have mightily increased in your *outward* Substance: May you equally increase in your *inward* Riches, and do good with both, while you have a Day to do Good. Your Enemies would once have taken what you had from you, *for His Name Sake*, in whom you have believed; wherefore He has given you much of the World, in the Face of your Enemies. But O let it be your *Servant*, and not your *Master!* Your *Diversion* rather than your *Business!* Let the Lord be chiefly in your Eye, and ponder your Ways, and see if God has nothing more for you to do: And if you find yourselves short in your Account with him, then wait for his Preparation, and be ready to receive the *Word of Command*, and *be not weary of well-doing*, when you have put your Hand to the *Plough*; and assuredly you shall *reap*, if you faint not, the Fruit of your Heavenly Labour in God's everlasting Kingdom.

And you *young convinced Ones*, be you intreated and exhorted to a *diligent* and *chaste* Waiting upon God, in the Way of his blessed Manifestation and Appearance of Himself to you. Look not

out

out but *within*: Let not another's Liberty be your *Snare*: Neither act by Imitation, but *Sense* and *Feeling* of God's Power in yourselves: Crush not the tender Buddings of it in your Souls, nor *over-run*, in your Desires and Warmness of Affections, the holy and gentle Motions of it. Remember it is a *still Voice*, that speaks to us in this Day, and that it is not to be heard in the *Noises* and *Hurries* of the Mind; but is distinctly understood in a *retired Frame*. Jesus *loved* and *chose* Solitudes; often going to *Mountains*, *Gardens* and *Sea-sides*, to avoid Crouds and Hurries, to shew His Disciples it was good to be *Solitary*, and sit *loose* to the World. Two Enemies lie near your *States*, *Imagination* and *Liberty*; but the plain, practical, living, holy Truth, that has convinced you, will preserve you, if you mind it in yourselves, and bring all Thoughts, Inclinations and Affections, to the Test of it, to see if they are wrought in God, or of the Enemy, or of your ownselves: so will a true *Taste*, *Discerning* and *Judgment*, be preserved to you, of what you should do and leave undone. And in your Diligence and Faithfulness in this Way you will come to inherit Substance; and Christ, the eternal Wisdom, will fill your *Treasury*. And when you are converted, as well as convinced, then *confirm* your Brethren; and be *ready* to every *good Word* and *Work*, that the Lord shall call you to; that you may be to His Praise, who has chosen you to be Partakers, with the Saints in Light, of a Kingdom that cannot be shaken, an Inheritance incorruptible in eternal Habitations.

And now, as for you, that are the Children of God's

God's *People*, a great Concern is upon my Spirit for your *Good*: And often are my Knees *bowed to the* God *of your Fathers, for you*, that you may come to be *Partakers* of the same divine Life and Power, that have been the Glory of this Day; that a *Generation* you may be to God, an *holy Nation*, and a *peculiar People, zealous of good Works*, when all our Heads are laid in the *Dust*. O! you *young Men and Women!* let it not suffice you, that you are the Children of the People of the Lord; you must also be *born again*, if you will inherit the Kingdom of God. Your Fathers are but such after the Flesh, and could but beget you into the Likeness of the *first Adam*; but you must be begotten in the Likeness of the *second Adam*, by a Spiritual Generation, or you will not, you cannot be of His Children or Offspring. And therefore *look carefully about you*, O ye Children of the Children of God! Consider your Standing, and see what you are in Relation to this divine Kindred, Family and Birth. Have *you obeyed the Light*, and received and walked in the Spirit, which is the incorruptible Seed of the Word and Kingdom of God, of which you must be born again. God is no Respecter of *Persons*. The Father cannot save or answer for the Child, or the Child for the Father, but in the Sin thou sinnest thou shalt die; and in the Righteousness thou dost, through Christ Jesus, thou shalt live; for it is the *Willing* and *Obedient* that shall eat the *Good* of the Land. *Be not deceived,* God *is not mocked*; *such as all Nations and People sow, such they shall reap at the Hand of the just God.* And then your many and great Privileges, above the Children of other People, will add

add Weight in the Scale against you, if you choose not the Way of the Lord. For you have had *Line upon Line*, and *Precept upon Precept*, and not only *good Doctrine*, but *good Example*; and which is more, you have been turned to, and acquainted with, a Principle in yourselves, which others too generally have been ignorant of: And you know you may be as good as you please, without the Fear of *Frowns* and *Blows*, or being *turned out of Doors*, and *forsaken of Father and Mother*, for God's *Sake* and His *holy Religion*, as has been the Case of some of *your Fathers*, in the Day they first entered *into his holy Path*. And if you, after hearing and seeing the *Wonders* that God has *wrought* in the Deliverance and Preservation of them, through a *Sea of Troubles*, and the manifold temporal, as well as spiritual Blessings that He has filled them with, in the Sight of their Enemies, should neglect and turn your Backs upon *so great and near a Salvation*, you would not only be most ungrateful Children to God and them, but must expect that God will call the Children of *those that knew him not*, to take the Crown out of your Hands, and that your Lot will be a dreadful Judgement at the Hand of the Lord: But O that it may never be so with any of you. *The* Lord *forbid,* saith my Soul.

Wherefore, O *ye young Men* and *Women,* look to the Rock of your Fathers: There is *no other* God *but Him, no other* Light *but His, no other* Grace *but His,* nor Spirit *but His,* to convince you, quicken and comfort you; to lead, guide and preserve you to God's everlasting Kingdom. So will you be Possessors as well as Professors of the Truth, embracing

ing it, not only by *Education*, but *Judgment* and *Conviction*; from a Sense begotten in *your Souls*, through the *Operation* of the eternal *Spirit* and *Power* of God; by which you may come to be the Seed of *Abraham*, through Faith, and the *Circumcision not made with Hands*; and so Heirs of the Promise made to the Fathers, of an *incorruptible Crown*: That, as I said before, *a Generation you may be to* God, holding up the Profession of the blessed Truth in the Life and Power of it. For *Formality* in Religion is *nauseous* to God and *good Men*; and the more so, where any Form or Appearance has been new and peculiar, and begun and practised, upon a Principle, with an *uncommon* Zeal and Strictness. Therefore I say, for you to fall flat and formal, and continue the Profession, without that Salt and Savour, by which it is come to obtain *a good Report among Men*, is not to *answer* God's *Love*, or your Parents Care, or the Mind of Truth in yourselves, or in those that are without: Who, tho' they will not obey the Truth, have Sight and Sense enough to see, if they do that make a Profession of it. For where the divine Virtue of it is not felt in the Soul, and waited for, and lived in, Imperfections will quickly break out, and shew themselves, and detect the Unfaithfulness of such Persons; and that their *Insides* are not seasoned with the Nature of that holy Principle which they profess.

Wherefore, *dear Children*, let me intreat you to *shut your Eyes* at the Temptations and Allurements of this low and perishing World, and not suffer your Affections to be captivated by those Lusts and Vanities that your Fathers, *for the Truth's Sake,*

Sake, long since turned their Backs upon: But as you believe it to be the Truth, receive it into *your Hearts*, that you may become the Children of God: So that it may never be said of you, as the *Evangelist* writes of the *Jews* in his Time, That Christ, the true Light *came to His own, but His own received Him not; but to as many as received Him, to them He gave Power to become the Children of God, which were born, not of Blood, nor of the Will of the Flesh, nor of the Will of Man, but of* God. A most close and comprehensive Passage to this Occasion. You *exactly* and *peculiarly* answer to those professing *Jews*, in that you bear the Name of God's People, by being the Children, and wearing of the Form of God's People: And He, by *His Light in you*, may be very well said to come to His own, and if you obey it not, but turn your back upon it, and walk after the *Vanities* of your Minds, you will be of those that received Him not, which I pray God may never be your Case and Judgment: But that you may be *throughly sensible* of the many and great Obligations you lie under to the Lord for His Love, and to your Parents for their Care: And with *all your Heart, and all your Soul, and all your Strength, turn to the* Lord, *to His Gift and Spirit in you, and hear His Voice and obey it, that you may seal to the Testimony of your Fathers, by the Truth and Evidence of your own Experience;* that your Children's Children may *bless you*, and the Lord *for you*, as those that deliver'd a *faithful Example*, as well as Record of the Truth of *God* unto them. So will the *grey Hairs* of your dear Parents, yet alive, *go down to the Grave with Joy*, to see you the Posterity of Truth, as well as theirs, and that not only

only their Nature but Spirit shall live in you when they are gone.

I shall conclude this Account with a few Words to those that are not of our Communion, into whose Hands this may come; especially those of our own Nation.

Friends, as you are the Sons and Daughters of *Adam*, and my Brethren after the Flesh, *often and earnest* have been my Desires and Prayers to God on your Behalf, that you may come to know your *Creator* to be your *Redeemer* and *Restorer* to the *holy* Image, that through Sin you have lost, by the Power and Spirit of His Son Jesus Christ, whom He hath given for the *Light* and *Life* of the World. And O, that you, who are called *Christians*, would receive him into *your Hearts!* For there it is you want Him, and at *that* Door He stands knocking that you might let Him in, but you do not open to Him: You are full of other Guests, so that a *Manger* is His Lot among you now, as well as of old. Yet you are full of Profession, as were the *Jews* when he came among them, who knew him not, but *rejected* and *evilly entreated* him. So that if you come not to the Possession and Experience of what you profess, all your Formality in Religion will stand you in *no Stead* in the Day of God's Judgment.

I beseech you *ponder* with yourselves your eternal Condition, and see what *Title*, what Ground, and Foundation you have for your *Christianity*: If more than a *Profession*, and an *Historical Belief* of the *Gospel?* Have you known the *Baptism of Fire*, and the *Holy Ghost*, and the *Fan* of Christ, that winnows away the *Chaff* in your Minds, the
carnal

carnal Lusts and *Affections?* That *divine Leaven* of the Kingdom, that, being received, leavens the *whole Lump* of Man, sanctifying him *throughout* in Body, Soul and Spirit? If this be not the Ground of your Confidence, you are in a miserable Estate.

You will say, perhaps, *That though you are Sinners, and live in daily Commission of Sin, and are not sanctified,* as I have been speaking, *yet you have Faith in* Christ, *who has borne the Curse for you, and in Him you are compleat by Faith, His Righteousness being* imputed *to you.*

But, my *Friends,* let me intreat you not to deceive yourselves, in so important a Point, as is that of your immortal Souls. If you have *true Faith* in Christ, your Faith will make you *clean*; it will sanctify you: For the Saints *Faith* was their Victory of old: By this they overcame *Sin within,* and *sinful Men without.* And if thou art in Christ, thou walkest not after the Flesh, *but after the Spirit,* whose Fruits are manifest. Yea, thou art a *new Creature*: New made, new fashioned; after God's Will and Mould. Old Things are done away, and behold, all Things are become new: *New Love, Desires, Will, Affections* and *Practices.* It is not any longer thou that livest; thou disobedient, carnal, Worldly One; but it is Christ *that liveth in thee*; and to live is Christ, and to die is thy eternal Gain: Because thou art assured, that thy Corruptible shall put on Incorruption, and thy Mortal, Immortality, and that thou hast a glorious House eternal in the Heavens that will never wax old or pass away. All this follows being in Christ, as *Heat* follows Fire and *Light* the Sun.

Therefore

Therefore have a Care how you presume to rely upon such a Notion, as that you are in Christ, *whilst in your old fallen Nature*. For what Communion hath Light with Darkness, or Christ with *Belial?* Hear what the beloved Disciple tells you; *If we say we have Fellowship with* God *and walk in Darkness, we lie, and do not the Truth*. That is, if we go on in a sinful Way, are captivated by our carnal Affections, and are not converted to God, we walk in Darkness, *and cannot possibly in that State have any Fellowship with* God. Christ *clothes them with His Righteousness, that receive His Grace in their Hearts, and deny themselves, and take up His Cross daily, and follow Him*. Christ's Righteousness makes Men *inwardly* holy; of holy Minds, Wills and Practices. It is nevertheless Christ's, because we have it; for it is ours, not by Nature, but by *Faith* and *Adoption:* It is the Gift of God. But still, though not ours, as of or from ourselves, for in that Sense it is Christ's, for it is of and from Him; yet it is ours, and must be ours in *Possession, Efficacy* and *Enjoyment*, to do us any *Good;* or Christ's Righteousness will profit us nothing. It was after this Manner that He was made, to the Primitive *Christians, Righteousness, Sanctification, Justification* and *Redemption;* and if ever you will have the *Comfort, Kernel* and *Marrow* of the *Christian* Religion, thus you must come to learn and obtain it.

Now, my *Friends*, by what you have read, you may perceive that God has visited a *poor People* among you with this saving Knowledge and Testimony: Whom He has upheld and encreased to
this

his Day, notwithstanding the fierce Opposition they have met withal. Despise not the Meanness of this Appearance: It was, and yet is (we know) a *Day of small Things*, and of small Account with too many; and many hard and ill Names are given to it: But it is of God, it came from Him because it leads to Him. This we know, but we cannot make another to know it, unless he will take the *same Way* to know it that we took. The World talks of God, but *what* do they do? They pray for Power, but *reject* the Principle in which it is. If you would know God, and worship and serve God as you should do, you must come to the Means he has ordained and given for that Purpose. Some seek it in *Books*, some in *learned Men*, but what they look for, is *in themselves*, though not *of* themselves, but they *overlook* it. The Voice is too still, the Seed too small, and the Light shineth in Darkness; they are abroad, and so cannot divide the Spoil: But the Woman that lost her Silver, found it at Home, after she had lighted her Candle and swept her House. Do you so too, and you shall find what *Pilate* wanted to know, *viz.* Truth. *Truth in the inward* Parts, so valuable in the Sight of God.

The Light of Christ within, who is the Light of the World, (and so a Light to you, that tells you the Truth of your Condition) leads all, that take Heed unto it, out of *Darkness into* God's *marvellous Light*. For Light grows upon the Obedient: *It is sown for the Righteous, and their Way is a shining Light, that shines forth more and more to the perfect Day*.

Wherefore, O *Friends*, turn in, turn in, I beseech

seech you: *Where* is the Poison, *there* is the Antidote. *There* you want Christ, and *there* you must find him; and, blessed be God, *there you may find Him. Seek and you shall find*, I testify for God. But then you must seek *aright*, with your *whole Heart*, as Men that seek for their *Lives*, yea, for their *eternal* Lives: Diligently, humbly, patiently, as those that can taste no Pleasure, Comfort or Satisfaction in any Thing else, unless you find Him whom your Souls want to know and love *above all*. O it is a Travail, a *spiritual Travail!* let the carnal, profane World, think and say as it will. And through *this Path* you must walk to the City of God, that has eternal Foundations, if ever you will come there.

Well! and *what does this* blessed Light *do for you?* Why, *first*, It sets all your Sins in Order before you: It detects the Spirit of this World in all its Baits and Allurements, and shews how Man came to fall from God, and the fallen Estate he is in. *Secondly*, It begets a *Sense* and *Sorrow*, in such as believe in it, for this fearful Lapse. You will then see him distinctly whom you have pierced, and all the *Blows* and *Wounds* you have given Him by your *Disobedience*, and how you have made him to serve with your Sins; and you will weep and mourn for it, and your Sorrow will be a *Godly* Sorrow. *Thirdly*, After this it will bring you to the *holy Watch*, to take Care that you do so no more, and that the Enemy surprise you not again. Then *Thoughts*, as well as Words and Works, will come to *Judgment*, which is the Way of Holiness, in which the Redeemed of the Lord do walk. Here you will come to love God above all, *and your Neighbours as yourselves.* Nothing *hurts,* nothing *harms,* nothing makes *afraid* on this holy Mountain. Now you come to be Christ's indeed; for you are His in *Nature* and *Spirit,* and not your own. And when you are thus Christ's then Christ is *yours,* and not before. And here Communion with the Father, and with the Son you will know, and the *Efficacy* of the Blood of Cleansing, even the Blood of Jesus Christ, that *immaculate Lamb,* which speaks better Things than the Blood of *Abel*; and which cleanseth from *all Sin* the Consciences of those that thro' the *living Faith* come to be *sprinkled* with it from *dead Works to serve the living* God.

To conclude, behold the *Testimony* and *Doctrine* of the People called *Quakers!* Behold their *Practice* and *Discipline!* And behold the *blessed Man* and *Men* (at least many of them) that were *sent* of God in this *excellent Work and Service!* All which is *more particularly expressed in the Annals* of that Man of God: Which I do *heartily recommend* to my *Readers* most *serious Perusal;* and *beseech Almighty* God, that His *Blessing* may go along with both, to the *Convincement of many,* as yet *Strangers* to this *holy Dispensation,* and also to the *Edification* of God's *Church in general:* Who for His *manifold and repeated Mercies and Blessings* to His *People in this Day of His great Love,* is *worthy* ever to have the *Glory, Honour, Thanksgiving* and *Renown;* and be it *rendered* and *ascribed,* with *Fear* and *Reverence,* thro' Him in whom He is *well pleased,* His beloved *Son* and *Lamb,* our *Light* and *Life,* that sits with Him upon the *Throne,* World without End. *Amen.*

Says

Says one that God *has long since mercifully favoured with His* Fatherly Visitation, *and who was not* disobedient *to the Heavenly Vision and Call; to whom the Way of Truth is more lovely and precious than ever, and that knowing the Beauty and Benefit of it above all* Worldy Treasures, *has chosen it for his* chiefest Joy; *and therefore recommends it to thy Love and Choice, because he is with great Sincerity and Affection,*

Thy Soul's Friend,

WILLIAM PENN.

F I N I S.

THE ANARCHY OF THE RANTERS,

And other LIBERTINES;

THE HIERARCHY OF THE ROMANISTS,

AND OTHER
Pretended CHURCHES, equally refused and refuted, in a two-fold *Apology* for the Church and People of God, called in Derision, *Quakers*.

WHEREIN

They are vindicated from those that accuse them of *Disorder* and *Confusion* on the one Hand, and from such as calumniate them with *Tyranny* and *Imposition* on the other; shewing, that as the true and pure *Principles* of the Gospel are restored by their Testimony; so is also the *antient Apostolic ORDER* of the Church of Christ re-established among them, and settled upon its right *Basis* and *Foundation*.

By ROBERT BARCLAY.

Phil. 2. 3. *Let nothing be done through Strife or vain Glory; but in Lowliness of Mind let each esteem other better than themselves.*
Heb. 13. 7. *Remember them that have the Rule over you, who have spoken unto you the Word of God, whose Faith follow.*

WILMINGTON,
Re-printed by JAMES ADAMS,
M,DCC,LXXXIII.

THE PREFACE TO THE READER.

SUCH *is the Malignity of Man's Nature in his fallen State, and so averse is he from walking in the* straight *and* even Path of TRUTH, *that at every Turn he is inclinable to lean either to the Right-hand or to the Left; yea, such as by the Work of God's Grace in their Hearts, and powerful Operation of his Spirit, have obtained an Entrance in this Way, are daily molested, and set upon, on all Hands; some striving to draw them the one Way, some the other: And if through the Power of God they be kept* faithful *and* stable, *then are they calumniated on both Sides; each likening or comparing them to the Worst of their Enemies.*

Those that are acquainted with the Holy Scriptures, *may observe this to be the Lot of the Saints in all Ages; but especially those, whose Place it hath been to* reform *and* restore *the Ruins of the House of God, when decayed: Hence those that set about repairing of the Walls of* Jerusalem, *were necessitated to work with the one Hand, and defend with the other.*

Christ is accused of the Jews *as a* Samaritan; *and by the* Samaritans *quarrelled with for being a* Jew. *The Apostle* Paul *is whipped and imprisoned by the* Gentiles, *and upbraided with being a* Jew, *and teaching their Customs; the same Paul is hawled, and ready to be killed by the* Jews, *for breaking the Law, and defiling the Temple with the* Gentiles. *The like hath also befallen these* faithful Witnesses *and* Messengers, *whom God has raised up in this Day to witness for his Truth, which hath long been in a great Measure hid; but now is again revealed, and many brought to be Witnesses of it, who thereby are come to* walk in the Light of the Lord.

This People thus gathered, have not wanted those Trials, that usually accompany the Church of Christ, both on the Right-hand and on the Left, each characterizing them in such Terms, as they have judged would prove most to their Disadvantage. From whence (as the Testimony of the false Witnesses against our Lord did not agree, neither do these against us) some will have us to be foolish mad Creatures ; *others to be* deep, subtil Politicians ; * *some to be* illiterate, ignorant Fellows ; *others to be* learned, cunning Jesuits, *under a meer Vizard:* Divers Professors *will have us to be only* Pensioners of the Pope, *undoubtedly* Papists ; *but the Papists abhor us as* Hereticks : *Sometimes we are a* disorderly, confused Rabble, *leaving every one to do as they list, against all good* Order *and* Government ; *at other Times we are so much for Order, as we admit not Men to exercise the Liberty of their own Judgments. Thus are our Reputations tossed by the Envy of our Adversaries; which yet cannot but have this Effect upon sober minded People, as to see what* MALICE *works against us ; and how these Men, by their contradictory Assertions concerning us, save us the Pains, while they* refute one another.

True it is, we have laboured to walk amidst these Extremities ; and upon our appearing for the Truth,

* *John Owen charges us with so much ignorance, that though he writes against us in* Latin, *he fears we will not understand it. And Thomas Danson about the same Time accuses us of being Jesuits, sent from abroad under this Vizard.*

we

we have found Things good *in themselves* abused on both Hands: *for such hath always been the Work of an* Apostacy, *to keep up the* Shadow *of certain* Truths; *that there-through they might shelter other* Evils. *Thus the* Jews *made Use of the Law and the Prophets to vindicate their* Abuses; *yea, and to crucify* Christ: *And how much many* Christians *abuse the* Scriptures *and the* Traditions *of the Apostles, to uphold Things quite contrary to them, will in the general be readily acknowledged by most.*

But to descend more particularly; There be two Things especially, both of which in their primitive Use were appointed; and did very much contribute towards the Edification of the Church: The one is,

I. The Power and Authority, which the Apostles had given them of Christ, for the gathering, building up, and governing of his Church; by Virtue of which Power and Authority they also wrote the Holy Scriptures.

II. *The other is,* That Privilege given to every Christian under the Gospel, to be led and guided by the Spirit of Christ, and to be taught thereof in all Things.

Now, both these in the Primitive-Church wrought effectually towards the same End of Edification; *and did (as in their Nature they may, and in their Use they ought to do) in a good Harmony very well consist together: But by the Workings of Satan, and Perverseness of Men, they are made to fight against and destroy one another. For on the one Hand the Authority and Power, that resided in the Apostles, while it is annexed and entailed to an outward Ordination and Succession of Teachers, is made Use of to cloak and cover all Manner of Abuses, even the Height of* Idolatry *and* Superstition. *For by Virtue of this Succession*

Succession these Men claiming the like Infallibility, *that was in the* Apostles *(though they be Strangers to any inward Work or Manifestation of the Spirit in their Hearts) will needs oblige all others to acquiesce and agree to their* Conclusions, *however different from, or contrary to, the Truths of the Gospel; and yet for any to call such Conclusions in Question, or examine them, is no less than a* henious Heresy, *deserving* Death, &c. *Or while the Revelation of God's Mind is wholly bound up to these Things already delivered in the Scriptures (as if God had spoke his* last Words *there to his People* *) *we are put with our own* natural Understandings *to debate about the Meanings of them, and forced to interpret them, not as they plainly speak, but according to the Analogy of a certain Faith made by Men, not so much contrived to answer the Scriptures, as the Scriptures are strained to vindicate it; which to doubt of, is also counted* Heresy, *deserving no less than Ejection out of our native Country, and to be robbed of the common Aid our Nativity entitles us to. And on this Hand, we may boldly say, both* Papists *and* Protestants *have greatly gone aside.*

On the other Hand, some are so great Pretenders to inward Motions *and* Revelations of the Spirit, *that there are no Extravagancies so wild, which they will not cloak with them; and so much are they for every One's following their own Mind, as can admit of no* Christian Fellowship *and* Community, *nor of that good* Order *and* Discipline, *which the Church of Christ never was, nor can be without. This gives an open Door to all* Libertinism, *and brings great Reproach to the Christian Faith. And on this Hand have foully fallen the* German Anabaptists, *so called,* John of Leyden,

* So faith *James Durham,* a noted Man among the *Presbyterians,* in his Exposition upon the *Revelations.*

Leyden, Knipperdolling, &c. *(in Case these monstrous Things committed by them, be such as they are related)* and *some more moderate of that Kind have been found among the* People *in* England, *called* Ranters: *As it is true, the People called* Quakers *have been branded with both of these Extreams; it is as true, it hath been and is their Work to avoid them; and to be found in that even and good Path of the* Primitive-Church, *where all were (no Doubt) led and acted by the Holy Spirit; and might all have* prophesied *one by one; and yet there was a* Subjection of the Prophets to the Spirits of the Prophets. *There was an* Authority *some had in the Church, and yet it was for* Edification, *and not for* Destruction: *There was an* Obedience in the Lord *to such as were set over; and a being taught by such, and yet a knowing of the* inward Anointing, *by which each Individual was to be led into all Truth. The Work and Testimony the Lord hath given us, is to restore this again, and to set both these in their right Place, without causing them to destroy one another. To manifest how this is accomplished, and accomplishing among us, is the Business of this Treatise; which, I hope, will give some Satisfaction to Men of sober Judgments, and impartial and unprejudicate Spirits; and may be made useful in the good Hand of the Lord, to confirm and establish Friends against their present Opposers; which is mainly intended, and earnestly prayed for, by*

ROBERT BARCLAY.

The 17th of the 8th
   Month, 1674.

THE

THE CONTENTS.

Section I. *THE Introduction and Method of this Treatise.*

Section II. *Concerning the Ground and Cause of this Controversy.*

Section III. *Whether there be any Order or Government in the Church of Christ.*

Section IV. *Of the Order and Government we plead for.*

Section V. *In what Cases, and how far, this Government extends.*

Section VI. *How far this Government extends in Matters spiritual, and purely conscientious.*

Section VII. *Concerning the Power of Decision.*

Section VIII. *How this Government altogether differeth from the Oppressing and Persecuting Principality of the Church of Rome, and other antichristian Assemblies.*

The CONCLUSION.

THE ANARCHY OF THE RANTERS, &c.

SECTION I.

The Introduction and Method of this Treatise.

AFTER that the Lord God in his own appointed Time had seen meet to put an End to the Dispensation of the Law, which was delivered to the Children of *Israel*, by the Ministry of *Moses*; through and by whom he did communicate unto them in the Wilderness from Mount *Sinai*, divers Commandments, Ordinances, Appointments and Observations, according as they are testified in the Writings of the Law; it pleased him to send his own Son the Lord Jesus Christ in the Fulness of Time; who having perfectly fulfilled the Law, and the Righteousness thereof, gave Witness to the Dispensation of the Gospel. And having approved himself, and the Excellency of his Doctrine, by many

[side note: The End of the Law and Beginning of the Gospel Dispensation recited.]

many great and wonderful Signs and Miracles, he sealed it with his Blood; and triumphing over Death (of which it was impossible for him to be held). He cherished and encouraged his despised Witnesses, who had believed in him, in that he appeared to them, after he was raised from the Dead; comforting them with the Hope and Assurance of the *pouring forth of his Spirit*, by which they were to be led and ordered in all Things; in and by which, He was to be with them to the End of the World, not suffering the Gates of Hell to prevail against them. By which Spirit come upon them, they being filled, were embolned to preach the Gospel without Fear; and, in a short Time, Thousands were added to the Church; and the Multitude of them that believed, were of one Heart, and of one Soul, and great Love and Zeal prevailed, and there was nothing lacking for a Season.

But all that were caught in the Net, did not prove good and wholesome Fish; some were again to be cast into that Ocean, from whence they were drawn: Of those many that were called, all proved not chosen Vessels, fit for the Master's Use; and of all that were brought into the great Supper and Marriage of the King's Son, there were that were found without the Wedding-Garment.---- Some made a shew for a Season, and afterwards fell away; there were that drew back; there were that made Shipwreck of Faith, and of a good Conscience: There were not only such as did backslide themselves, but sought to draw others

The divers Sorts of them that were called in the Apostles Days.

others into the same Perdition with themselves, seeking to overturn their Faith also; yea, there were that brought in damnable Heresies, even denying the Lord that bought them. And also of those Members that became not wholly corrupt (for some were never again restored by Repentance) there were that were weak, and sickly, and young; some were to be fed with Milk, and not with strong Meat; some were to be purged, when the old Leaven received any Place; and some to be cut off for a Season, to be shut out (as it were) of the Camp for a Time, until their Leprosy was healed, and then to be received in again.

Moreover, as to *Outwards*, there was the Care of the Poor, of the Widow, of the Fatherless, of the Strangers, &c. Therefore the Lord Jesus Christ, who is the Head of the Body, the Church (for the Church is the Body of Christ, and the Saints are the several Members of that Body) knowing, in his infinite Wisdom, what was needful for the good ordering and disposing all Things in their proper Place, and for preserving and keeping all Things in their right Station, did, in the Dispensation and Communication of his Holy Spirit, minister unto every Member, a *Measure of the same Spirit*, yet diverse according to Operation, for the Edification of the Body; some Apostles, some Teachers, some Pastors, some Elders: There are old Men, there are young Men, there are Babes. For all are not Apostles, neither are all Elders, neither are all Babes; yet are all Members: And as such, all

(marginal note: The Order in the Church of God in the Outward.)

all have a Sense and Feeling of the Life of the Body, which from the Head, flows unto all the Body, *as the Ointment of* Aaron's *Beard, unto the Skirts of his Garment:* And every Member has its Place and Station in the Body, so long as it keeps in the Life of the Body; and all have Need one of another; yet is no Member to assume another Place in the Body than God has given it; nor yet to grudge or repine its Fellow Member's Place; but to be content with its own: For the uncomely Parts are no less needful than the comely; and the less honourable than the more honourable; which the Apostle *Paul* holds forth in 1 *Cor.* 12. from Verse 13 to 30.

<small>The Ground of Rents and Divisions.</small> Now the Ground of all Schisms, Divisions or Rents in the Body is, when as any Member assumes another Place than is allotted it; or being gone from the Life and Unity of the Body, and losing the Sense of it, lets in the Murmurer, the Eye that watches for Evil, and not in holy Care over its Fellow Members: And then, instead of coming down to *Judgment in itself,* will stand up and *judge its Fellow Members,* yea, the whole Body, or those whom God has set in a more honourable and eminent Place in the Body than itself. Such suffer not the Word of Exhortation; and term the Reproofs of Instruction (which is the Way of Life) *Imposition* and *Oppression,* and are not aware how far they are in the Things they condemn others for; while they spare not to reprove and revile all their Fellow Members: Yet if they be but admonished

nished themselves, they cry out, as if their great Charter of Gospel Liberty were broken.

Now though such, and the Spirit by which they are acted, be sufficiently seen and felt by Thousands, whose Hearts God has so established, as they are out of Danger of being intangled in that Snare, and who have Power and Strength in themselves to judge that Spirit, even in its most subtil Appearances; yet there are, who cannot so well withstand the Subtilty, and seeming Sincerity some such pretend to, though in Measure they have a Sight of them; and others, that cannot so rightly distinguish between the Precious and the Vile; and some there are that through Weakness, and Want of true Discerning, may be deceived, and the Simplicity in them betrayed for a Season; as it is written, *With fair Speeches and smooth Words, they deceive the Hearts of the Simple*.

The Subtilty of that Spirit.

Therefore having, according to my Measure, received an Opening in my Understanding as to these Things, from the Light of the Lord, and having been for some Time under the weighty Sense of them, I find at this Instant a Freedom to commit them to Writing, for the more universal Benefit and Edification of the Church of Christ.

Now for the more plain and clear Opening and Understanding of these Things, it is fit to sum up this Treatise in these following general Heads, to be considered of:

The Heads treated of, viz.

First,

I.   First, *From whence the Ground and Cause of this Controversy is, the Rise and Root of it?*

II.   Secondly, *Whether there be now any Order and Government in the Church of Christ?*

III.   Thirdly, *What is the Order and Government which we plead for?*

In what Cases, and how far it may extend? In whom the Power decisive is, and how it differeth? And is wholly another, than the oppressing and persecuting Principality of the Church of Rome, *and other Antichristian Assemblies.*

SECTION II.

Concerning the Ground and Cause of this CONTROVERSY.

The first Dawning of the heavenly Day of the Lord described.

WHEN as the Lord God by his mighty Power began to visit the Nations with the Dawning of his heavenly Day (for thus I write unto those that have received and believed the Truth) and that he sent forth his Instruments, whom he had fitted and prepared for his Work, having fashioned them not according to the Wisdom and Will of Man, but to his own heavenly Wisdom and Counsel, they went forth and preached the Gospel in the Evidence and Demonstration of the Spirit: Not in the enticing Words of Man's Wisdom; but in Appearance

And breaking forth.

ance as Fools and Mad, to those that judged according to Man. But their Words and Testimony pierced through into the inner Man in the Heart, and reached to that of God in the Conscience; whereby as many as were simple-hearted, and waited for the Redemption of their Souls, received them as the Messengers of the most high God; and their Words were unto them, not as the Words of Men, but as the Words of God; for in the receiving and embracing the Testimony of Truth through them, they felt their Souls eased, and the acceptable Day began to dawn in and upon them.

Now what Evidence brought these Men to make their Testimony to be received? Did they entice? Did they flatter? Did they daub up? Did they preach Liberty to the Flesh or Will of Man? Nay verily, they used no such Method: Their Words were as Thunder-Bolts, knocking down all that stood in their Way, and pouring down the Judgment of God upon the Head of the Transgressor every where. Did they spare the zealous Professor more than the open Profane? Nay verily, they condemned equally the Hypocrisy of the one, as well as the Profanity of the other; yet wanted they not Regard to the tender Seed and Plant of God in either. Did they give way? Did they yield to the Wisdom of Man? To the Deceitfulness of the Serpent, that would reason Truth for themselves, saying, *I must stay until I be convinced of this, and that, and the other Thing; I see not yet this to be wrong, or the other Thing to be my Duty?* How did they knock down this Manner of Reasoning by the Spirit of God, which
wrought

wrought mightily in them, shewing and holding forth, that this is the Day of the Lord that is dawned; that all are invited to come; that none ought to tarry behind; that that which so pleadeth is the same Spirit which of old Time said in those that were invited, *I cannot come yet, I must first marry a Wife; I must go prove my Yoke of Oxen; I must go visit my Possessions; let me first bury my dead Father.* Did not the Lord through them testify and declare against these Things? And is there not a Cloud of Witnesses, who felt the Enemy thus reasoning to keep us in the Forms, Fellowships, false Worships, and foolish Fashions of this World? But we felt, as we were obedient, all these Things to be for Condemnation; and that, as we obeyed the pure Manifestation of the Light of Jesus in our Hearts, there was no Hesitation. We might and should have parted with all those Things at the First; and what occasioned such Scruples, was but that which drew back, through being unwilling to give pure Obedience to the Cross of Christ: For as many as gave Obedience and believed in the Light, found no Occasion of stumbling; but such as believed not were condemned already, because they believed not in him that appeared. Now the Boldness, and Courage, and Efficacy of these Messengers Testimony, wrought such Astonishment, Fear, and Amazement in the Hearts of such as were ingenuous, that many began to be inwardly pricked, as in the Days of old, and the Foundations of many began to be shaken; and some that were asleep were awakened, and many that

The Courage of the Messengers.

that were dead and buried in the Graves of Sin, and Formality, and Superstition, and Idolatry of all Sorts, were alarmed ; and many were brought in from the Hedges, and the High-Ways, and the Truth was received by Thousands with great Cheerfulness, and a Readiness of Mind : And the Feet of those were beheld to be beautiful upon the Mountains, that brought the glad Tidings of these good Things. And great Lowliness and Simplicity of Heart was upon such that were newly convinced of the Truth, and deep Humiliation of Spirit, and Subjection to the Power, both in themselves, and in those who were over them in the Lord, and had gathered them into the Truth.

But as it was in the Gatherings of old, so it also fell out in this Day ; all kept not their first Love : As among those Thousands, which *Moses* led out of *Egypt*, and carried through the *Read Sea*, who had sung Praises to God upon the Banks of Salvation, many Carcases fell in the Wilderness ; some who murmured and longed to return again to the Flesh-Pots of *Egypt* ; and some for opposing and contradicting the Servant, and Servants of the Lord, whom the Lord had made Use of to lead them out of Bondage, in saying, *Ye take too much upon you* ; *Hath the Lord indeed only spoken by* Moses ? *Hath he not spoken also by us?* And as among these Multitudes which were gathered by the Apostles, there were many who continued not faithful to the End ; some returned back again with the Sow to the Puddle after they were washed ; some embraced the present World ; some again separated themselves, being sensual, and without the

Opposition and ——

——Separation entering.

Spirit,

Spirit, *despising Dominions, and speaking Evil of Dignities*; their Mouths speaking great swelling Words, being puffed up, and not abiding in these Things, which they were taught of the Apostles: So it is to be lamented, that among these many Thousands, whom the Apostles and Evangelists whom God raised up in *this* Day (for the gathering of his Seed and People out of spiritual *Egypt* and *Babylon* into his pure Light and Life) did bring forth and gather, there are that have fallen upon the Right-hand and the Left. Some are turned back again into *Egypt*, running into the same Excess of Lust and Riot, from whence they were once purified and redeemed: Some could not bear the Reproach of the Cross of Christ; and were by and anon offended in him: Some could not bear the Tribulations, Sufferings and Persecutions, which came for the Truth's Sake; and the Seed in them was soon scorched with the Heat of the Day. And some not abiding in Subjection to the Truth in themselves, were not contented with that Place and Station in the Body, which God had placed them in; but became vainly puffed up in their fleshly Minds, intruding into those Things which they had not seen: And would needs be *Innovators*, given to Change, and introducing new Doctrines and Practices, not only differing, but contrary to what was already delivered in the Beginning;

Innovators causing Divisions.

making Parties, causing Divisions and Rents, stumbling the Weak, and denying, despising and reviling the Apostles and Messengers of Christ, the Elders of the Church, who loved not their Lives unto Death, but through much Care, and Travel,

The Controversy Stated.

Travel, and Watchings, and Whippings, and Bonds, and Beatings, in daily Jeopardy, gathered us by the mighty Power of God into the most precious Truth. Yet in all this there hath nothing befallen us, but that which hath been the antient Lot of the Church of Christ in the primitive Times.

Now He, that was careful for his Church and People in old Times, hath not been wanting to us in our Day; but as he has again restored the Truth unto its primitive Integrity and Simplicity, and as he has delivered our Understandings from these false Doctrines and Principles, which prevailed in the Apostacy; so he hath not gathered us to be *As Sheep scattered without a Shepherd*, that every one may run his own Way, and every one follow his own Will, and so to be as a confused Mass or Chaos, without any Order; but He, even the *LORD* hath also gathered, and is gathering us into the *good Order, Discipline, and Government of his own Son, the Lord Jesus Christ*: Thereforth he hath laid Care upon some beyond others, *who watch for the Souls of their Brethren, as they that must give Account*. <small>The good Shepherd of *Israel's* Care over his Church and People.</small>

There are then Fathers that have begotten us unto Christ Jesus through the Gospel, of whom we ought to be Followers, and to remember their Ways, which be in Christ. There are then Fathers and Children, Instructors and Instructed, Elders and young Men, yea, and Babes; there are that connot cease, but must exhort, instruct, reprove, condemn, judge; <small>The several Stations in the Church. 1 Cor. 4. 15, 16, 17.</small>

or else, for what End gave Christ the Gifts mentioned, *Ephes.* 4. 11, 12? And how are the Saints perfected, and the Body of Christ edified of those, who came under the Cognizance, and, as it were, the Test of this Order and Government? I may chiefly sum them up in three Sorts (though there be divers other little subdivided Species of them.)

1. Prophane backsliding Apostates.

The First is *Those that turn openly back to the World again*, through finding the Way of Truth too narrow. These have not been capable to do us any considerable Hurt; for being a Salt, that has lost its Savour, they mostly prove a Stink among those to whom they go. And I never knew any of them, that proved any ways steady among those to whom they go. I find other Professors make but small Boast of any Proselytes they got out from among us: I hear little of their proving Champions for the Principles of others against us. And, indeed, for the most Part they lose all Religion with the Truth: For I have heard some of them say; *That if ever they took on them to be religious, they would come back again to the* Quakers, *&c.*

2. Unwary repenting Sinners.

Secondly, Those, who through Unwatchfulness, the secret Corruption of their own Hearts, and the mysterious or hidden Temptations of the Enemy, have fallen into his Snares; and so have come under the Power of some Temptation or other, either of fleshly Lusts, or of spiritual Wickedness: Who being seasonably warned by those that keep their Habitation, and faithful Overseers feers in the Church; have been again restored by unfeigned Repentance: Not kicking against the Pricks; but have rejoiced, that others watched over them for their Good, and are become Monuments of God's Mercy unto this Day.

Thirdly, Such, who being departed from their first Love and antient Zeal for the Truth, become cold and lukewarm; and yet are ashamed to make open Apostacy, and to turn back again, so as to deny all the Principles of Truth, they having had already such Evidence of Clearness upon their Understanding: Yet not keeping low in their own Habitations, but being puffed up, and giving way to the restless Imaginations of their exalted and wandering Minds, fall out with their Brethren; cause Divisions; begin to find fault with every Thing, and to look at others more than at themselves; with swelling Words to talk of, and preach up, a higher Dispensation, while they are far from living up to the Life and Perfection of this present; like unto such who said, *We will not have this Man to rule over us:* Cry out of Formality and Apostacy, because they are not followed in all Things; and if they be reproved for their Unruliness, according to the good Order of the Church of Christ, then they cry out, *Breach of Liberty, Oppression, Persecution! we will have none of your Order and Government; we are taught to follow the Light in our Consciences, and not the Orders of Men.* Well, of this hereafter; but this gave the Rise of this Controversy: Which leads me to that which I proposed in the second Place.

Margin note: 3. Self-Separating troublesome Opposers.

SECTION

Section III.

Whether there be now to be any Order *or* Government *in the* Church *of* Christ.

IN Answer to this *Proposition*, I meddle not at this Time with those that deny any such Thing as a Church of Christ; I have reserved their Plea to another Place. Neither need I to be at much Pains to prove the Affirmative, to wit, *That there ought to be Government and Order in the Church of Christ* unto the Generality of our Opposers, both *Papists* and *Protestants*; who readily confess and acknowledge it, and have heretofore blamed us for Want of it. Tho' now some of them, and that of the highest Pretenders, are become so unreasonable, as to accuse us for the Use of it; improving it, so far as they can, to our Disadvantage: For such is the Blindness of partial Envy, that whereas the supposed Want of it was once reckoned heritical, now the present Performance of it is counted criminal.

<small>Church Order and Government granted.</small>

These, then, to whom I come to prove this Thing, are such, who having cast off the Yoke of the Cross of Christ in themselves, refuse all *Subjection* or *Government*: Denying that any such Thing ought to be, as disagreeing with the Testimony of Truth: Or those, who not being so wilful and obstinate in their Minds, yet are fearful or scrupulous in the Matter, in respect of the dangerous Consequences, they may apprehend, such a Thing may draw after it.

For

For the clearing then as well the Mistakes of the one, as answering the Cavils of the other, I judge the Truth of these following Assertions will sufficiently prove the Matter; which I shall make no great Difficulty to evidence.

First, *That Jesus Christ, the King and Head of the Church, did appoint and ordain, that there should be Order and Government in it.*   Reason I.

Secondly, *That the Apostles, and primitive Christians, when they were filled with the Holy Ghost, and immediately led by the Spirit of God, did practise and commend it.*   II.

Thirdly, *That the same Occasion and Necessity now occurring, which gave them Opportunity to exercise that Authority, the Church of Christ hath the same Power now as ever, and are led by the same Spirit into the same Practices.*   III.

As to the *First*, I know there are some, that the very Name of a Church, and the very Words, Order and Government they are afraid of. Now this I suppose hath proceeded, because of the great Hypocrisy, Deceit and Oppression, that hath been cloaked with the Pretence of these Things; but why should the Truth be neglected, because Hypocrites have pretended to it? The right Institution of these Things, which have been appointed and ordained of God, must not, nor ought not to be despised, because corrupt Men have abused and perverted them. I know not any Thing that hath been more abused and perverted in the whole World, than the Name of a Christian; shall we then renounce that honourable Title, because so many Thousands

The Abuse makes not void the true Use.

lands of wicked Men, yea, Antichrists have falsly assumed it to themselves? The Man of Sin hath taken upon him to sit in the Temple of God, as God; yet we must not therefore deny, *that God is in this Temple.* If the Synagogue of Satan assumed the Name of the Church of Christ, and hath termed her Oppression and Violence, the Power and Authority thereof; therefore must not the Church of Christ, and its Authority, be exercised, where it truly is according to his Mind? This I prefix to warn all to beware of stumbling at Things which are innocent in themselves; and that we may labour to hold the steady even Path of Truth, without running into either of the Extremes. For that Jesus Christ did appoint Order and Government to be in the Church, is very clear from his plain Words, *Matt.*

Church Order appointed by Christ, & the Form thereof.

Chap. 18. Ver. 15. *Moreover, if thy Brother shall trespass against thee, go tell him his Fault between thee and him alone; if he shall hear thee, thou hast gained thy Brother.* Ver. 16. *But if he will not hear thee, then take with thee one or two more, that in the Mouth of two or three Witnesses, every Word may be established.* Ver. 17. *And if he shall neglect to hear them, tell it unto the Church: But if he neglect to hear the Church let him be unto thee as an Heathen-Man, and a Publican.* Ver. 18. *Verily, I say unto you, whatsoever ye shall bind on Earth, shall be bound in Heaven; and whatsoever ye shall loose on Earth, shall be loosed in Heaven.* From which Scripture it

I. doth manifestly and evidently follow, *First,* That Jesus Christ intended there should be certain Order and Method in his Church, in the Procedure towards such as transgress. *Secondly,* That he that refuseth to hear two, is become more guilty (as hardned) than in refusing to hear him that first reproved alone. *Thirdly,* That refusing to hear the Judgment of the Church, or whole Assembly, he doth thereby exclude himself, and shut out himself from being a Member; and is justly judged, by his Brethren, as an Heathen and a Publican.

II.

III.

And *Lastly,* that the Church, Gathering or Assembly of God's People, has Power to examine and call to Account such as, appearing to be among them, or owning the same Faith with them, do transgress; and in case of their refusing to hear, or repent, to exclude them from their Fellowship: And that God hath a special Regard to the Judgment and Sense of his People thus orderly proceeding, so as to hold such bound in Heaven, whom they bind on Earth, and such loosed in Heaven, whom they loose on Earth. I am partly confident, that no rational Man will deny, but that these naturally follow from the above-mentioned Scripture; and if there should be any found so unreasonable as to deny it, I could prove it by necessary and unevitable Consequences; which at present, as taking it for granted, I forbear to do. If it be reckoned so great a Crime to *offend one of the little Ones,* that it were better for him, that so do, that a *Millstone were hanged about his Neck, and he were drowned in the Depth of the Sea;* without Question, to offend and gainsay the whole Flock, must be more criminal,

IV.

criminal, and must draw after it a far deeper Judgment.

Now if there were no Order nor Government in the Church, what should become of those that transgress? How should they be again restored? Would not this make all Reproving, all Instructing, all Caring for, and Watching over one another, void and null? Why should Christ have desired them to proceed after this Method? Why doth he place so much Weight upon the Judgment of the Church, as to make the refusing of hearing it, to draw so deep a Censure after it; which he will not have to follow the refusing to hear one or two apart, though the Matter be one and the same? And so, as to the substantial and intrinsick Truth of the Thing, there lies the same Obligation upon the Transgressor to hear that one, as well as all; for that one adviseth him to that which is right and good, as well as the Whole; and they do but homologate or confirm that which that one hath already asserted: Yet Jesus Christ, who is the Author of Order, and not of Confusion, will not have a Brother cut off, or reputed a *Publican*, for refusing to hear one or two, but for refusing to hear the Church. And if it be objected, *That the Church of* Rome, *and all other false Churches, make Use of this Scripture, and cover their Persecution, and Cruelty, and Oppression by it; and thou sayest no more than they say.* I answer; I suppose no Man will be so unreasonable as to affirm, that the Church of *Rome* abusing this Scripture, will make

make it false in itself; but how we differ in our Application of this Scripture, shall be spoken of hereafter. I am not now claiming Right to this Power, as due to us (that is reserved for another Place;) but this, I say, is that which I now aver to be manifest from the Scripture-Testimony, and to be in itself an unquestionable Truth, *That Jesus Christ intended there should be Order and Government in his Church*; which is the Thing at present in Hand to be proved: Which if it be so really true (as it cannot be denied) then I hope it will also necessarily follow, that such who really and truly are the Church of Christ, have Right to exercise this Order and Government.

Secondly, That the Apostles and Primitive-Christians, did practise Order and Government, we need but read the History of the *Acts*, of which I shall mention a few pregnant and undeniable Testimonies, as we may observe in the very first Chapter of the *Acts*, from Verse 13. to the End, where at the very first Meeting the Apostles and Brethren held together after the Ascension of Christ, they began orderly to *appoint one* to supply the Place of *Judas*; it may be thought, this was a needless Ceremony; yet we see how the Lord countenanced it. I hope none will say, that the Apostles appointing of these two Men, or him, upon whom the Lot did not fall, contradicted their inward Freedom, or imposed upon it; but both agreed very well together; the one in the Will and Movings of God

<small>Reason II. Church Order practised by the Apostles & primitive Christians.---In Elections.</small>

God in appointing, and the other in the same, in submitting to their Appointment.

Moreover, after they had received the Holy Ghost, you may read, *Acts* 6. so soon as there was an Opportunity, how they wisely gave Order, concerning the Distribution for the Poor, and appointed some Men for that Purpose. So here was Order and Government, according to the present Necessity of the Case: And the Lord God was well pleased with it, and the Word of God increased, and the Number of the Disciples multiplied in *Jerusalem* greatly. Might they not have said then, as some say now; *We will give our Charity to whom we see Cause; and we will take no Notice of your Appointments and Orders:* Whether would God have approved of such, yea, or nay?

Thirdly, When that the Business of Circumcision fell in, whether it was fit or not to circumcise the *Gentiles?* We see, the Apostles saw not meet, *To suffer every one to follow their own Minds and Wills:* They did not judge, as one confusedly supposeth, *That this Difference in an outward Exercise, would commend the Unity of the true Faith:* Nay, they took another Method. It is said expresly, *Acts* 15. 6. *And the Apostles and Elders came together, to consider of this Matter; and after there had been much disputing about it,* (no Doubt then there were here Diversities of Opinions and Judgments) the Apostles and Elders told their Judgments, and came also to

positive

---in Distributions for the Poor.

W. M. in his Queries.

--in Differences occuring.

positive Conclusion. Sure some behoved to submit, else they should never have agreed. So those that were the Elders, gave a positive Judgment; and they were bold to say, *That it pleased not only them but the Holy Ghost.* By all which it doth undeniably appear, that the Apostles, and primitive Saints, practised a Holy Order and Government among themselves: And I hope none will be so bold as to say, they did these Things without the Leadings of the Spirit of God, and his Power and Authority concurring, and going along with them.

And that these Things were not only singular Practices, but that they held it doctrinally; that is to say, it was Doctrine which they preached; that there ought to be Order and Government in the Church, is manifest from these following Testimonies, 1 *Cor.* 4. 15, 16, 17. *(15.) For though you have Ten Thousand Instructors in Christ; yet have ye not many Fathers; For in Christ Jesus, I have begotten you through the Gospel. (16.) Wherefore I beseech you, be ye Followers of me. (17.) For this Cause have I sent unto you* Timotheus, *who is my beloved Son, and faithful in the Lord; who shall bring you into Remembrance of my Ways, which be in Christ, as I teach every where in every Church.* Here the Apostle Paul is very absolute: *First*, In that he desires them to be *Followers* of him. *Secondly*, In that he sends a Teacher, yea, a Minister, and eminent Bishop, or Overseer of the Church, for to put them in Mind of his *Ways*, which be in *Christ*,

The Apostles Doctrine concerning Order in the Church.

1 Cor. 4. 15, 16, 17.

as

as he taught in every Church. No Doubt there were Apostates, and dissenting Spirits in the Church of *Corinth*, that gave *Paul* Occasion thus to write, as he testifies in the Beginning of the Chapter, how he was *judged by some of them*; he shews, how they were *grown high*; Verse 8. *Now ye are full, now ye are rich, ye have reigned as Kings without us,* &c. Might not these Dissenters of the Church of *Corinth*, have reasoned thus against *Paul?* Did not this *Paul* teach us, at first, to mind the *Measure of Grace in ourselves*, and follow that? (for no Doubt that was *Paul*'s Doctrine) But now he begins to lord it over us, and tells us, we must be *Followers of him.* Might they not have judged the beloved *Timothy* to be far out of his Place? might they not have said, It seems it is not God that moved thee, and sent thee here by his Spirit; but lordly *Paul*, that seeks Dominion over our Faith: It seems thou comest not here to preach Christ, and wish us to be Followers of him, and of his Grace in our Hearts; but to mind us to follow *Paul*'s Ways, and take Notice, how he *teaches in every Church:* We are not concerned with him, nor with his Messenger, nor with any of your Orders, and so forth. Doth not this run very plausible? I question not but there was such a Reasoning among the Apostate *Corinthians*; let such as are of the same Kind among us examine seriously, and measure their Spirits truly hereby. Yea, he goes yet further in the following Chapter,

Marginal note: Dissenting Reasonings against Church-Government.

Verses 3, 4. *Verse 3. As absent in Body, but present in Spirit, I have judged already, as though I were present, concerning him that hath so done the Deed. Verse 4. In the Name of our Lord Jesus Christ, when ye are gathered together, and my Spirit with the Power of our Lord Jesus Christ,* &c. Would not one think this to have been a very *presumptuous Word?* And yet who dare offer to condemn it? From all which, I shall shortly observe, that it seems it was judged no *Inconsistency* nor *Contradiction,* to be *Followers of the Grace in themselves, to be perswaded in their own Hearts, and also to be Followers of the Apostle* Paul, *and of his Ways;* because his Ways and Example was no other than the Spirit of God in themselves would have led them to, if they had been obedient: Therefore he found it needful to charge 'em positively to *follow him,* without adding this Reason.

1 Cor. 5. 3--13. The Power of giving Judgment in the Church.---

Next, the great Argument the Apostle uses to perswade them hereunto, upon which he mainly insists, because he had begotten them into the Truth; *Ye have not many Fathers; for in Christ Jesus, I have begotten you through the Gospel: Wherefore I beseech you, be ye Followers of me.* So he makes that as the Cause; which the same Apostle also in his Expostulation with the *Galatians,* putting them in Mind how he preached the Gospel to them at first, and Chap. 4. Ver. 15. *Where is then the Blessedness ye spake of? For I bear you Record, if possible ye would have*

-As of Fathers.

have plucked out your own Eyes, and given them unto me. We see then, that the Lord hath, and doth give such, whom he hath fur-
—And Overseers. nished, and sent forth to gather a People unto himself, Care and Oversight over that People; yea, and a certain Authority in the Power over them to bring them back to their Duty, when they
--To be obeyed. stray at any Time; and to appoint, yea, and *command* such Things as are needful for *Peace*, and *Order*, and *Unity*'s Sake: And that there lies an *Obligation* upon such as are so gathered, to *reverence, honour*, yea, and *obey* such as are set over them in the Lord. For, saith the same Apostle, 2 *Cor.* 2. 9. *For to this End also did I write, that I might know the Proof of you, whether you be obedient in all Things*: And Chap. 7. Ver. 13. 15. *Yea, and exceedingly the more joyed we for the Joy of Titus, because his Spirit was refreshed by you all.* Ver. 1

Betrayings of the Enemy.
And his inward affection is more abundant towards you, whilst he remembereth the Obedience of you all, how with Fear and Trembling ye received him.

Now this will not at all infer, as if they had been implicitly led of old: Or that such, as having the same Authority to exercise it now, sought Dominion over their Brethren's *FAITH*, or to force them to do any Thing beyond, far less contrary to, what the Lord leads us to by his Spirit: But we know (as they did of old) that the Enemy lies near to *BETRAY* under such Pretences. And seeing, in case of Difference, the

the Lord hath, and doth, and will reveal his Will to his People, and hath, and doth raise up Members of his Body, to whom he gives a Discerning, and Power, and Authority to instruct, reprove, yea, and command in some Cases, those that are faithful and low in their Minds, keeping their own Places, and minding the Lord, and the Interest and Good of his *Truth* in the general over all, shut out the Murmurer; and the Spirit of God leads them to have Unity, and concur with their Brethren. *The Murmurer shut out.* But such as are heady and high-minded, are inwardly vexed, that any should lead or rule, but themselves: And so it is the high Thing in themselves, that makes them quarrel with others for taking so much upon them; pretending a Liberty, not sinking down in the Seed to be willing to be of no Reputation for its Sake. Such, rather than [giv]e up their own Wills, will study to make [Re]nts and Divisions, not sparing the [F]lock; but prostrating the Reputation and Honour of the Truth even to the World, minister to them an Occasion of Scorn and Laughter, to *The Honour of Truth prostrated by Divisions.* the hardening them in their Wickedness and Atheism.

Besides these Scriptures mentioned, I shall set down a few of many more that might be instanced to the same Purpose.

Ephes. 5. 21. *Submitting yourselves one to another in the Fear of God.* *Scriptures for Submission, & Lowliness of Mind; and Esteem of the Brethren.*

Phil. 2. 3. *Let nothing be done through Strife or vain Glory, but* in *Lowliness of Mind, let each esteem other better than themselves.*

Verse 29. *Receive him therefore in the Lord with all Gladness, and hold such in Reputation.*

And 3. 17. *Brethren, be Followers together of me; and mark them which walk so, as ye have us for an Ensample.*

And 4. 9. *Those Things, which ye have both learned, and received, and heard, and seen in me, do; and the God of Peace shall be with you.*

Col. 2. 5. *For though I be absent in the Flesh, yet am I with you in the Spirit, joying and beholding your Order, and the Stedfastness of your Faith in Christ.*

1 Thess. 5. 12. *And we beseech you, Brethren, to know them which labour among you, and are over you in the Lord, and admonish you.*

Verse 13. *And to esteem them very highly in Love, for their Work's Sake; and be at Peace among yourselves.*

Verse 14. *Now we exhort you, Brethren, w[arn] them that are unruly, comfort the feeble Minded, support the Weak, be patient toward all Men.*

2 Thess. 2. 15. *Therefore, Brethren, stand fast, and hold the Traditions which you have been taught, whether by Word, or our Epistle.*

2 Cor. 10. 8. *For though I should boast somewhat more of our Authority (which the Lord hath given us for Edification, and not for your Destruction) I should not be ashamed.*

Now though the *Papists* greatly abuse this Place, as if hereby they could justify that Mass of Superstition, which they have heaped together; yet except we will deny the plain Scripture, we

Church-Order and Government Asserted. 27

we must needs believe, there lay an Obligation upon the *Thessalonians* to observe and hold these Appointments, and no Doubt, needful Institutions, which by the Apostles were recommended unto them: And yet who will say, that they ought, or were thereby commanded to do any Thing contrary to that which the Grace of God in their Hearts moved them to?

2 Thess. 3. 4. *And we have Confidence in the Lord touching you, that ye both do, and will do the Things which we command you.*

Verse 6. *Now we command you, Brethren, in the Name of our Lord Jesus Christ, that ye withdraw yourselves from every Brother that walketh disorderly, and not after the Tradition which he received of us.*

What more positive than this? and yet the Apostle was not here an Imposer. And yet further, Verse *The Authority of the Church no Imposition.*

And if any Man obey not our [Wo]rd by this Epistle, note that Man, and have no Company with him, that he may be ashamed.

Thus, Heb. 13. 7. *Remember them which have the Rule over you, who have spoken unto you the Word of God, whose Faith follow; considering the End of their Conversation.*

Verse 17. *Obey them that have the Rule over you, and submit yourselves; for they watch for your Souls, as they that must give Account: That they may do it with Joy, and not with Grief; for that is unprofitable for you.*

Jude 8. *Likewise also these filthy Dreamers defile the Flesh, despise Dominion, and speak Evil of Dignities.*

I 2   I might

I might at Length enlarge if needful, upon these Passages, any of which is sufficient to prove the Matter in Hand; but that what is said may satisfy such as are not wilfully blind and obstinate. For there can be nothing more plain from these Testimonies, than that the *antient Apostles and primitive Christians practised Order and Government in the Church*; that some did appoint and ordain certain Things; condemn and approve certain Practices, as well as Doctrines, by the Spirit of God: That there lay an Obligation in Point of Duty upon others to obey and submit:: That this was no Encroachment nor Imposition upon their Christian Liberty; nor any Ways contradictory to their being inwardly and immediately led by the Spirit of God in their Hearts: And lastly, That such, as are in the true Feeling and Sense, will find it their Places to obey, and be one with the Chu[rch] of Christ in such like Cases: And that it is su[ch] as have lost their Sense and Feeling of the Li[fe] of the Body, that dissent, and are disobedient, under the false Pretence of Liberty. So that thus it is sufficiently proved what I undertook in this Place.

The primitive Christians practised Order in the Church.

Thirdly, I judge there will need no great Arguments to prove the People of God may, and do well to exercise the like Government upon the very like Occasion. For even Reason may teach us, that what proved good and wholesome Cures to the Distemper of the Church in former Ages, will not now (the very like Distempers falling in) prove hurtful

Reason III.

and poisonable; especially, if *we have the Testimony of the same Spirit in our Hearts; not only allowing us, but commanding us so to do.* It is manifest (though we are sorry for it) that the same Occasions now fall in; we find that there are that have eaten and drunken with us at the Table of the Lord, and have been Sharers of the same spiritual Joy and Consolation, that afterwards fall away. We find (to our great Grief) that some walk disorderly; and some are puffed up, and strive to sow Division, labouring to stumble the Weak, and to cause Offences in the Church of Christ: What then is more suitable, and more christian, than to follow the Foot-steps of the Flock, and to labour and travel for the Good of the Church, and for the removing all that is hurtful; even as the Holy Apostles, who walked with Jesus, did before? If there be such that walk disorderly now, must not they be admonished, rebuked and withdrawn from, as well as of old? Or is such to be the Condition of the Church in these latter Times, that all Iniquity must go unreproved? Must it be Heresy, or Oppression, to watch over one another, in Love? To take Care for the Poor? To see that there be no corrupt, no defiled Members of the Body, and carefully and christianly deal with them, for restoring them, if possible; and for withdrawing from them, if incurable? I am perswaded, that there are none that look upon the Commands of Christ and his Apostles, the Practice and Experience of the primitive Church and Saints, as a sufficient

Distempers of the Church require a Cure now as of old.

Prece-

Precedent to authorize a Practice now, that will deny the Lawfulness or Usefulness hereof, but must needs acknowledge the Necessity of it. But if it be objected (as some have done)

Objection. do not you deny that the Scripture is the adequate Rule of Faith and Manners; and that the Commands or Practices of the Scripture are not a sufficient Warrant for you now to do any Thing, without you be again authorized, and led unto it by the same Spirit? And upon that Score, do you not forbear some Things both *practised* and *commanded* by the primitive Church and Saints?

Well, I hope I have not any Thing weakened this *Objection*, but presented it in its full Vigour and Strength: To which I shall clearly and distinctly answer thus.

Times alter the Usefulness of Things commanded. *First*, Seasons and Times do not alter the Nature and Substance of Things in themselves; though it m[ay] cause Things to alter, as to the Usefulness, or not Usefulness of them.

Secondly, Things commanded and practised at certain Times and Seasons fall of themselves, when as the Cause and Ground, for which they were commanded, is removed, as there is no Need now for the Decision about *Circumcision*, seeing there are none contend for it: Neither as to the Orders concerning Things offered to Idols, seeing there is now no such Occasion: Yet who will say, that the Command enjoined in the same Place, *Acts* 15. 20. *To abstain from Fornication*, is now made void; seeing there is daily Need for its standing in Force, because it yet remains

as

as a Temptation Man is incident to? We confess, indeed, we are against such as from the bare Letter of the Scripture (though if it were seasonable now to debate it, we find but few to deal with, whose Practices are so exactly squared) seek to uphold *Customs*, *Forms* or *Shadows*, when the Use, for which they were appointed, is removed or the Substance itself known and witnessed; as we have sufficiently elsewhere answered our Opposers in the Case of *Water-baptism*, and *Bread* and *Wine*, &c. So that the *Objection*, as to that, doth not hold; and the Difference is very wide, in Respect of such Things: The very Nature and Substance of which can never be dispensed with by the People of God, so long as they are in this World; yea, without which they could not be his *People*. For the Doctrines, and fundamental Principles of the Christian Faith, we own and believe originally and principally, because they are the *Truths* of God; whereunto the Spirit of God in our Hearts hath constrained our Understandings to obey and submit. In the second Place, we are greatly confirmed, strengthened and comforted in the *joint Testimony* of our Brethren, the Apostles and Disciples of Christ, who by the Revelation of the same Spirit in the Days of old believed, and have left upon Record the same Truths; so we *having the same Spirit of Faith*, according as it is written, *I believed, and therefore have I spoken*; we also believe, and therefore we speak. And we deny not but some, that from the Letter have had the Notion of these Things,

The joint Testimony of the Apostles, &c. to the Truths of God in our Hearts.

Things, have thereby in the Mercy of God received Occasion to have them revealed in the *Life:* For we freely acknowledge (though often calumniated to the Contrary) that *whatsoever Things were written aforetime, were written for our Learning; that we through Patience and Comfort of the Scriptures may have Hope.* So then I hope, if the Spirit of God lead me now unto that which is good, profitable, yea, and *absolutely needful,* in order to the keeping my Conscience clear and void of Offence towards God and Man, none will be so unreasonable as to say, I ought not to do it, *because it is according to the Scriptures.* Nor do I think it will *favour ill* among any serious, solid Christians, for me to be the more confirmed and perswaded that I am led to this Thing by the Spirit, that I find it in myself *good* and *useful;* and that upon the like Occasions Christ *commanded* it, and the Apostles and primitive Christians practised and recommended it.

Now, seeing it is so that we can boldly say, with a good Conscience in the Sight of God, that the same Spirit, which leads us to believe the Doctrines and Principles of the Truth, and to hold and maintain them again, after the Apostacy, in their primitive and antient Purity, as they were delivered by the Apostles of Christ in the Holy Scriptures; I say, that the same Spirit doth now lead us into the like Holy Order and Government to be exercised among us, as it was among them, being now the like Occasion and Opportunity ministred to us; therefore, what can any christianly or rationally object against it? For that there is a real Cause for it, the Thing

Thing itself speaketh; and that it was the Practice of the Saints and Church of old, is undeniable: What Kind of Ground then can any such Opposers have (being such, as scrupling at this, do notwithstanding acknowledge our Principle) that this were done by Imposition or Imitation, more than the Belief of the Doctrines and Principles? Seeing as it is needful to use all Diligence to convince and perswade People of the Truth, and bring them to the Belief of it (which yet we cannot do, but as Truth moves and draws in their Hearts) it is also no less needful, when a People is gathered, to keep and preserve them in Unity and Love, as becomes the Church of Christ; and to be careful, as saith the Apostle, *That all Things be done decently, and in Order*; and that all that is wrong be removed, according to the Method of the Gospel; and the Good cherished and enduraged. So that we conclude, and that upon very good Grounds, *That there ought now, as well as heretofore, to be Order and Government in the Church of Christ*.

A real Cause for the same Order.

That which now cometh to be examined in the third Place is,

Head III.

First, *What is the Order and Government we plead for?*

1.

Secondly, *In what Cases, and how far it may extend? And in whom the Power decisive is?*

2.

Thirdly, *How it differeth, and is wholly another than the oppressive and persecuting Principality of the Church of* Rome, *and other Antichristian Assemblies?*

SECTION

Section IV.

Of the Order *and* Government *which we plead for.*

IT will be needful then, before I proceed to describe the *Order* and *Government* of the *Church*, to confider what is or may be properly underftood by the *Church:* For fome (as I touched before) feem to be offended, or at leaft afraid of the very Word; becaufe, *The Power of the Church, the Order of the Church, the Judgment of the Church,* and fuch like Pretences, have been the great Weapons wherewith Antichrift and the apoftate Chriftians have been thefe many Generations perfecuting the Woman, and warring againft the Man-child. And, indeed, great Difputes have been among the *learned Rabbies,* in the Apoftacy concerning this *Church*, what it is, or what may be fo accounted; which I find not my Place at prefent to dive much in, but fhall only give the true Senfe of it, according to Truth, and the Scriptures plain Teftimony.

What the Word *CHURCH* fignifies properly.

The Word *CHURCH* in itfelf, and as ufed in the Scriptures, is no other but a *Gathering Company,* or *Affembly of certain People, called or gathered together:* For fo the *Greek* Word fignifies;) which is that the Tranflators render *Church*) which Word is derived from the Verb *Evoco, I call out of,* from the Root *Voco, I call.* Now though the *Englifh* Word *Church* be only taken in fuch a Senfe, as People are *gathered together upon a religious Account;*

yet

yet the *Greek* Word, that is so rendered, is taken in general for every *Gathering*, or *Meeting together of People:* And therefore where it is said, *The Town Clerk of the* Ephesians *dismissed the Tumult, that was gathered there together*, the same *Greek* Word is used, *Acts* 19. 41. *He dismissed the Assembly* (or the *Church.*) *(dimisit Concionem.)*

A *Church*, then, in the Scripture-Phrase, is no other than a Meeting or Gathering of certain People, which (if it be taken in a religious Sense, as most commonly it is) are gathered together in the Belief of the same Principles, Doctrines and Points of Faith, whereby as a Body they become distinguished from others, and have a certain Relation among themselves; and a conjunct Interest to the maintaining and propagating these Principles they judge to be right: And therefore have a certain Care and Oversight over one another, to prevent and remove all Occasions that may tend to break this their conjunct Interest, hinder the Propagation of it, or bring Infamy, Contempt, or Contumely upon it; or give such as on the other Hand are, or may be banded together to undo them, just Occasion against them, to decry and defame them. *What a religious Church is.*

Now the Way to distinguish that *Church*, *Gathering*, or *Assembly* of People, whereof Christ truly is the Head, from such as falsely pretend thereto, is by considering the Principles and Grounds upon which they are gathered together, the Nature of that Hierarchy and Order they have among themselves, the Way and Method they *How to distinguish the true Church from the false.*

they take to uphold it, and the Bottom upon which it ftandeth; which will greatly contribute to clear all Miftakes.

Forafmuch as *Sanctification* and *Holinefs* is the great and chief End among true Chriftians, which moves them to gather together; therefore the Apoftle *Paul* defines the Church in his Salutation to the *Corinthians,* 1 Cor. 1. 2. *Unto the Church of God which is at* Corinth, *them that are fanctified in Chrift Jefus, called to be Saints.* So the Church is fuch as are fanctified in Chrift Jefus, called to be Saints.

The Church's Care over its Members, &c.

The Power and Authority, Order and Government we fpeak of, is fuch, as a *Church Meeting, Gathering* or *Affembly* claims towards thofe that have, or do declare themfelves Members, who own, believe and profefs the fame Doctrines and Principles of Faith with us, and go under the fame Diftinction and Denomination; whofe Efcapes, Faults and Errors may by our Adverfaries juftly be imputed to us, if not feafonably and chriftianly reproved, reclaimed or condemned. For we are not fo foolifh, as to concern ourfelves with thofe who are not of us; far lefs, who ftand in Oppofition to us, fo as to reprove, inftruct, or reclaim them, as Fellow-Members or Brethren: Yet, with a Refpect to remove the general Reproach from the Chriftian Name, with a tender Regard to the Good of their immortal Souls, for the Zeal we owe to God's Glory, and for the Exaltation and Propagation of his everlafting Truth and Gofpel in the Earth, we have not been wanting, with the Hazard of our

our Lives, to seek the scattered Ones, holding forth the living and sure Foundation, and inviting and perswading all to obey the Gospel of Christ, and to take Notice of his Reproofs, as he makes himself manifest in and by his Light in their Hearts. So our Care and Travel is, and hath been towards those that are without, that we may bring them into the Fellowship of the Saints in Light; and towards those that are brought in, that they might not be led out again, or drawn aside, either to the Left-hand, or the Right, by the Workings and Temptations of the Enemy.

These Things being thus cleared and opened, we do positively affirm, That we being *a People gathered together by the Power of God* (which most, if not all of those, that arising among ourselves do oppose us herein, have acknowledged) into the Belief of certain Principles and Doctrines, and also certain Practices and Performances, by which we are come to be separated and distinguished from others, so as to meet apart, and also to suffer deeply for our joint Testimony; there are and must of Necessity be, as in the gathering of us, so in the preserving of us while gathered, Diversities of Gifts and Operations for the edifying of the whole Body. Hence, *Diversities of Gifts in the Church.* saith the Apostle, 1 *Tim.* 5. 17. *Let the Elders, that rule well, be counted worthy of double Honour, especially they who labour in the Word and Doctrine:* And this we suppose neither to be *Popish*, nor Antichristian, let our Opposers say it as oft as they can, without reckoning the Apostles such. *Secondly,*

Secondly, Forasmuch as all are not called in the same Station, some rich, some poor; some Servants, some Masters, some married, some unmarried; some Widows, and some Orphans, and so forth; it is not only convenient, but absolutely needful, that there be cer-

Meetings about Business.

tain Meetings at certain Places and Times, as may best suit the Conveniencies of such, who may be most particularly concerned in them; where both those that are to take Care may assemble, and those who may need this Care, may come and make known their Necessities, and receive Help, whether by Counsel or Supply, according to their respective Needs. This doth not at all contradict the Principle of being led

---established by the Apostles.

inwardly and immediately by the Spirit; else how came the Apostle in that Day of the powerful pouring forth of the Spirit of God, to set apart Men for this Purpose? Sure, this was not to lead them from their inward Guide; yea, on the Contrary, it is expresly said, *Acts* 6. 3. *Look ye out among you seven Men of honest Report, full of the Holy Ghost, and Wisdom, whom we may appoint over this Business.* Sure, they were not to undertake a Business, being full of the Holy Ghost, which might import a Contradiction to their being led by it: So we see it is both fit and suitable to the Apostles Doctrine, to have *Meetings about Business.* Now if any should be so whimsical or conceited, as to scruple their being at set Places and Times, though these be nothing relative to the essential Parts, but only Circumstances, re-

lating

lating to the Conveniency of our Perfons; (which we muft have Regard to, fo long as we are cloathed with Flefh and Blood: And fuch Notionifts, as are againft this godly Care, work far more in their vain Imaginations, than they reduce to Practice; being like unto fuch of whom the Apoftle *James* teftified, who content themfelves, with faying to the Naked, *be cloathed; and to the Hungry, be fed*; while they offer not, in the leaft, to minifter to them thofe Things which are needful for cloathing and feeding of them:) Yet fhall we not fcruple to make it appear, that it is not without very good Ground that we both appoint Places and Times. And firft, as to the *Place*, I fay as before, it is with our Bodies we muft meet, as well as with our Spirits; and fo, of Neceffity, we muft convey our Bodies unto one Place, that we may fpeak and act in thofe Things we meet for: And that muft be in fome certain Place, where all muft know where to find it; having herein a Regard to the Conveniencies and Occafions of fuch as meet. Were it fit, that thofe of the Church of *Corinth* fhould go do their Bufinefs at *Antioch*, or the Church of *Jerufalem* at *Rome?* Nay furely, God hath not given us our Reafon to no Purpofe; but that we fhould make Ufe of it for his Glory, and the Good of our Brethren, yet always in Subjection to his Power and Spirit. And therefore we have Refpect to thefe Things in the appointing of our Meetings, and do it not without a Regard to the Lord, but in a Senfe of his Fear. And fo the like as to

Convenient Places to meet in---

Times,

Times, which is no contradicting of the inward Leading of the Spirit. Elſe how came the Apoſtle to appoint a Time to the *Corinthians* in their Contributions, deſiring them, 1 *Cor.* 16. 2. *To lay by them in Store upon the firſt Day of the Week*; yea, ſaith he not, *that he gave the ſame Order to the Church of* Galatia. I know not how any in Reaſon can quarrel about *ſet Times* for outward Buſineſs, it being done in a Subjection to God's Will, as all Things ought to be; or elſe how can ſuch as ſo do, but quarrel with the Apoſtle for this Impoſition (at that Rate) upon the Churches of *Corinth* and *Galatia?* We appoint no ſet Times for the Performance of the Worſhip of God, ſo as to appoint Men to preach and pray at ſuch and ſuch ſet Times; though we appoint Times to *meet together in the Name of the Lord*, that we may feel his Preſence, and he may move in and through whom he pleaſeth, without Limitation. Which Practice of *Meeting together*, we are greatly encouraged to by the Promiſe of Chriſt, and our own bleſſed Experience; and alſo we are ſeverely prohibited to lay it aſide by the Holy Apoſtle; and alſo, on the other Hand, by the ſad Experience of ſuch as by Negligence or Prejudice forſake the Aſſemblies of God's People; upon many of which is already fulfilled, and upon others daily fulfilling, the Judgments threatened upon ſuch Trangreſſors: Read *Heb.* 10. from Verſe 23, to the End, where that Duty is ſo ſeriouſly exhorted to, and the Contempt of

—And convenient ſet Times appointed.

Reaſons for the Continuance of our ſaid Practices.

it

it reckoned a wilful Sin, almoſt (if not altogether) unpardonable; yea, a *treading under Foot the Son of God, and a doing Deſpight to the Spirit of Grace*; which is fulfilled in our Day, and proves the lamentable Fruits of ſuch as have ſo back-ſlidden among us. And therefore having ſo much good and real Ground, for what we do herein, together with the Approbation and Encouragement of Chriſt, and his Apoſtles, both by Command and Practice, we can (as that both the *Alpha* and *Omega*, the Foundation and Cap-ſtone required) faithfully affirm in good Conſcience, *That God hath led us by his Spirit, both to appoint Places and Times, where we may ſee the Faces one of another; and to take Care one for another, provoking one another to Love and good Works.* And our Faith and Confidence herein cannot be ſtaggered by a meer Denial in our Oppoſers, which no Man of Conſcience and Reaſon will ſay it ought; seeing the Thing itſelf hath ſuch a ſolid and real Cauſe and Foundation, ſo good and ſuitable a Pattern and Example, and that it is conſtantly confirmed to us, both by the Teſtimony of God's Spirit in our Hearts, and by the good Fruits and Effects which we daily reap thereby, as a Seal and Confirmation that God is well pleaſed therewith, and approveth us in it.

Having thus far proceeded to ſhew that there ought to be Order and Government among the People of God, and that that which we plead for is, That there may be certain Meetings ſet apart for that *End*; it is next to be conſidered, *In what Caſes, and how far it may extend.*

K   SECTION

SECTION V.

In what Cases, and how far this Government *extends. And first, as to* Outwards *and* Temporals.

<small>The Occasion of these Meetings about Business.</small>

I Shall begin with that, which gave the first Rise for this *Order* among the Apostles; and I do verily believe, might have been among the first Occasions that gave the like among us, and that is, *The Care of the Poor; of Widows and Orphans. Love* and *Compassion* are the great, yea, and the chiefest Marks of Christianity: *Hereby shall it be known,* saith Christ, *that ye are my Disciples, if ye love one another.* And *James* the Apostle places Religion herein in the first Place; *Pure Re-*

<small>1. To take Care for the poor Widows and Orphans.</small>

ligion (saith he) *and undefiled before God and the Father is, to visit the Fatherless and Widows in their Afflictions, &c.* For this then, as one main End, do we meet together, that Enquiry may be made, if there be any Poor of the Houshold of Faith that need, that they may be supplied; that the Widows may be taken Care of; that the Orphans and Fatherless may be bred up and educated. Who will be so Unchristian, as to reprove this good *Order* and *Government,* and to say it is needless? But if any will thus object, *May not the Spirit lead every one of you to give to them that need? What needs meeting about it, and such Formalities?*

I answer,

I answer, The Spirit of God leads us so to do; what can they say to the contrary? Nor is this a Practice any Ways inconsistent with being inwardly and immediately led by the Spirit; for the Spirit of God doth now, as well as in the Days of old, lead his People into those Things which are orderly, and of a good Report; for he is the God of Order, and not of Confusion: And therefore the holy Apostles judged it no Inconsistency with their being led by the Spirit, to appoint *Men full of the Holy Ghost, and of Wisdom, over the Business of the Poor.* Now if to be *full of the Holy Ghost* be a Qualification needful for this Employment; surely the Nature of their Employment was not to render this so needful a Qualification useless and ineffectual, as if they were not to be led by it.

The Example of the Apostles.

Moreover we see, though they were at that Time all filled with the Spirit, yet there was something wanting before this good Order was established. *There was a Murmuring that some Widows were neglected in the daily Ministration;* and we must not suppose the Apostles went about to remedy this Evil that was creeping into the Church, without the Counsel of God by his Spirit; or that this Remedy they were led to, was stepping into Apostacy; neither can it be so said of us, we proceeding upon the like Occasion.

If then it be thus needful and suitable to the Gospel, to relieve the Necessities of the Poor, that as there was *no Beggar to be among Israel of old,* so far less now; must there not be

Contributions for the Poor.

be Meetings to appoint Contributions, in order to the performing these Things? Which is no other, but the giving of a general Intimation what the Needs are, that every one, as **God** moves their Hearts, and hath prospered them (without Imposition, Force, or Limitation) may give towards these needful Uses. In which Case these Murmurers at our good Order in such Matters, may well think strange at the Apostle: How pressingly! how earnestly doth he reiterate his Desires and Provocations, so to speak, in this Respect to the *Corinthians*, 1 *Cor.* 16. 2. and the eighth and ninth Chapters of the second Epistle throughout!

Now, though he testifies to them elsewhere, That *they are the Temples of the Holy Ghost, and that the Spirit of God dwells in them*; yet ceaseth he not to intreat and exhort, yea, and to give them certain Orders in this Matter.

Besides all these Reasons, which are sufficient to convince any unprejudicate Man, the secret Approbation of God's Spirit accompanying us in this Thing, together with the Fruits and Effects of it; which Hundreds can witness to, whose Needs have been supplied, and themselves helped through divers Difficulties; and the Testimonies of some already, and of many more Orphans and Fatherless Children, who have found no Want, neither of Father nor Mother, or other Relations, through the tender Love and Care of God's People, in putting them to Trades and Employments, and giving them all needful Education: Which will make it appear, ere this

<small>Fatherless Children put Apprentices.</small>

this Age pass away to those that have an Eye to see, that these are not the meer Doings and Orders of Men; but the *Work of him who is appearing in ten Thousands of his Saints, to establish not only Truth, but Mercy and Righteousness in the Earth.*

And for that End therefore in the second Place this Order reacheth the making up and composing of Differences as to outward Things, which may fall out betwixt Friend and Friend; for such Things may fall out through the Intricacies of divers Affairs, where neither hath any positive Intention to injure and defraud his Neighbour, as in many Cases might be instanced. Or if thro' the Workings and Temptations of him, whose Work is to beset the Faithful, and People of the Lord, and to engender (so far as he can) Strife and Division among them, any should so step aside as to offer to wrong or prejudice his Neighbour; we do boldly aver, as a People gathered together by the Lord, unto the same Faith, and distinguished from all others by our Joint-Testimony and Sufferings, that we have Power and Authority to decide and remove these Things among ourselves, without going to others to seek Redress. And this in itself hath so much Reason, that I cannot tell if any, that are not wholly prejudicate or obstinate, can blame it. For if we be of one Mind concerning Faith and Religion, and that it be our Joint-Interest to bring all others unto the same Truth with us, as supposing them to be wrong, what Confidence can we have to think of reclaiming them, if the Truth we profess have

2. To compose Differences in the Church, in outward Matters.

not such Efficacy, as to reconcile us among ourselves in the Matters of this World: If we be forced to go out to others for Equity and Justice, because we cannot find it among ourselves, how can we expect to invite them to come among us, when such Virtues, as which still accompany the Truth, are necessarily supposed to be wanting? Should we affirm otherwise, it were to destroy the Truth and Faith we have been, and are, in the Lord's Hand, building up: And indeed the Spirit and Practice of such as oppose us herein, hath no less Tendency.

Moreover, besides the enforcing and intrinsick Reason of this Thing, we have the Concurrence, Approbation and Comfort of the Apostle's Testimony, 1 *Cor.* 6. *Dare any of you, having a Matter against another, go to Law before the Unjust, and not before the Saints?* If it be objected, *Do you reckon all unjust that are not of you? Think ye all other People void of Justice?*

Objection.

Believers not to go to Law before the Unjust, &c.

I answer, Though the Apostle useth this Expression, I am persuaded he did not reckon all others unjust, that had not received then the Christian Faith. There were, no Doubt, moral and just Men among the *Heathen*; and therefore the same *Paul* commends the Nobility of *Festus*. He here reckons them *Unjust* in respect of the Saints, or comparatively with them, as such as are not come to the *just Principle of God in themselves*, to obey it and follow it: And therefore though he accounts them, who are least esteemed in the Church, capable to decide such Matters; yet

yet he supposeth it safer to submit to their Judgment in such Cases, though it were by *taking Wrong*, or *suffering Wrong*, than to go before others, to the greater Reproach of the Truth. We hope, though many Occasions of the Kind have fallen in among us, since we have been a People, none have had just Occasion to decline our Judgment. And though some should suppose themselves to be wronged; yet if they should bring their Matter before others, we might say, as the Apostle saith in the fore-mentioned Chapter, Ver. 7. *This were thereby a Fault in them*, and would evidence a greater Care of some outward Concern, than of the Honour and Interest of Truth; and therefore such as have a tender Regard that Way, would rather suffer what, to their Apprehensions, may seem wrong. For in Matters wherein two Parties are opposite in the Case of *Meum* and *Teum*, it is somewhat hard to please both; except where the Power of Truth, and the righteous Judgment thereof reaching to that of God in the Conscience, hath brought to a true Acknowledgment him that hath been mistaken, or in the Wrong; which hath frequently fallen out among us, to the often refreshing and confirming our Souls in the certain Belief, that Christ was fulfilling his Promises among us, *In restoring Judges, as at the first, and Counsellors, as in the Beginning*.

The Case of *Meum* and *Teum*.

Now, suppose any should be so pettish, or humorous, as not to agree in such Matters to the Judgment of

Going before Unbelievers from the Judgment of the Brethren, is a Dishonour to the Truth.

his

his Brethren, and to go before the Unbelievers (for though I reckon them not such Unbelievers as the *Heathen* of old, because they profess a Faith in God and Christ; yet I may safely say, they are Unbelievers as to these Principles and Doctrines, which we know are the Truth of God; and in that Sense must be Unbelievers as to him, that so appealeth to them from his Brethren.) I say, such as so do, first commit a certain Hurt, and Evil, in staining the Honour and Reputation of the Truth they profess, which ought to be dearer to us than our Lives. And even in that outward Matter, for which they thus do, they run a Hazard, not knowing whether Things shall carry, as they expect: If they lose, they have a double Prejudice; if they gain, it is at too dear Rate, even with the Hurt of *Truth's* Reputation, which their outward Advantage cannot make up. If then it be unlawful *to do Evil, that Good may come of it*, even a *Spiritual Good*; far less is it lawful to do a *Positive Evil*, of so deep a Dye as to bring an evil Report upon the good Land, and give the Uncircumcised an Occasion to rejoice: Out of the uncertain Hope of an outward Gain, it is far better to suffer Loss; as the Apostle very well argues in the Place above mentioned.

Indeed, if there be any such, who have been, or appear to be of us, as suppose, *There is not a wise Man among us all, nor an honest Man, that is able to judge betwixt his Brethren*; we shall not covet to meddle in their Matter, being perswaded, that either they, or their Cause, is nought.---
Though (Praises to God) among all those that
have

have gone from us, either upon one Account or other, I never heard that any were so minded towards us; but the most Part of them having let in the Offence of some Things, or Persons, have had this unanimous Testimony concerning us, that *generally we are an honest and upright-hearted People.* Apostates Testimony concerning us.

But whatever Sense our Enemies, or Apostates have of us, who look asquint, on the Face of *Truth,* and can see nothing aright in those they love not, or are prejudicate against: This we can say, in the last Place, (besides the Reasons and Scripture above declared) that the good Fruits, and Effects, which daily abound to the Houshold of Faith, in this, as well as the other Parts of the Government the Lord is establishing among us, doth more and more commend it unto us; and confirmeth our Hearts in the certain Belief of that, which we can confidently testify in good Conscience, *That God hath led us hereunto by his Spirit*; and we see the Hand of the Lord herein, which in due Time will yet more appear; that as through our faithful Testimony in the Hand of the Lord that antichristian and apostatized Generation, the NATIONAL MINISTRY, hath received a deadly Blow by our discovering and witnessing against their forced Maintenance, and Tythes, against which we have testified by many cruel Sufferings of all Kinds, (as our *Chronicles* shall make known to Generations to come) so that their Kingdom, in the Hearts of Thousands, begins to totter Priests forced Maintenance and Tythes have receiv'd a deadly Blow.

totter and lose its Strength, and shall assuredly fall to the Ground, through *Truth*'s prevailing in the Earth; so on the other Hand do we, by coming to Righteousness and Innocency, weaken the Strength of their Kingdom, who judge for Rewards (as well as such as preach for Hire) and by not ministring Occasion to those, who have heaped up Riches, and lived in Excess, Lust and Riot, by feeding and preying upon the Iniquities and Contentions of the People. For as Truth and Righteousness prevails in the Earth, by our faithful witnessing and keeping to it, the Nations shall come to be eased and disburdened of that deceitful Tribe of *Lawyers* (as well as *Priests*) who by their many Tricks and endless Intricacies, have rendred Justice, in their Method, burdensome to honest Men, and seek not so much to put an End, as to foment Controversies and Contentions, that they themselves may be still fed and upheld, and their Trade kept up. Whereas by Truth's Propagation, as many of these Controversies will die by Mens coming to be less contentious; so when any Difference ariseth, the Saints giving Judgment without Gift or Reward, or running into the Tricks and endless Labyrinths of the Lawyers, will soon compose them. And this is that we are perswaded the Lord is bringing about in our Day, though many do not, and many will not see it; because it is indeed in a Way different and contrary to Mens Wisdom, who are now despising Christ in his inward Appearance, because of the Meanness of it, as the *Jews* of old did

<small>Lawyers, by Tricks and Intricacies, foment Controversies.</small>

did him in his outward: Yet notwithstanding there were some then that did witness, and could not be silent, but must testify that *He was come*; even so now are there Thousands that can set to their Seal, that he hath now again the *second Time appeared*, and is appearing in *Ten Thousands of his Saints*; in and among whom (as a first Fruits of many more that shall be gathered) he is restoring the Golden Age, and bringing them into the Holy Order and Government of his own Son, who is ruling, and to rule in the midst of them, setting forth the Counsellors as at the Beginning, and Judges as at First; and establishing Truth, Mercy, Righteousness and Judgment again in the Earth: *Amen, Hallelujah!*

Christ's restoring the Golden Age.

Thirdly, These Meetings take Care in the Case of Marriages, that all Things be clear; and that there may be nothing done in that Procedure, which afterwards may prove to the Prejudice of Truth, or of the Parties concerned; which being an outward Thing (that is acknowledged in itself to be lawful) of the greatest Importance a Man or Woman can perform in this World; and from the sudden, unwary, or disorderly Procedure whereof, very great Snares and Reproaches may be cast both upon the Parties, and the Profession owned by them; therefore it doth very fitly, among other Things, when it occurs, come to be considered of by the People of God, when met, to take Care to preserve all Things right and savoury in the Houshold of Faith. We do believe our Adversaries, that watch

3. *To take Care in the Case of Marriages.*

watch for Evil against us, would be glad how promiscuously or disorderly we proceeded in this weighty Matter, that so they might the more boldly accuse us, as Overturners of all human and Christian Order: But God hath not left us without his Counsel and Wisdom in this Thing; nor will he, that any should receive just Occasion against us his People: And therefore in this weighty Concern, we, who can do nothing against the Truth, but all for, and with Regard to the Truth, have divers Testimonies for the Lord. And---

1. Our Testimony against marrying with the Unbelievers. Firſt, *That we cannot Marry with those that walk not in, and obey not the Truth, as being of another Judgment, or Fellowship; or pretending to it, walk not suitably and answerable thereto.*

2. By the Priest. Secondly, *Nor can we go to the Hireling-Priests, to uphold their false and usurped Authority, who take upon them to marry People without any Command, or Precedent for it from the Law of God.*

3. In forbidden Degrees. Lastly, *Nor can we suffer any such Kind of Marriages to pass among us, which either as to the Degrees of Consanguinity, or otherwise, in itself is unlawful, or from which there may be any just Reflection cast upon our Way.*

Test. 1. Against Unbelievers. As to the first Two, they being Matter of Principles received and believed, it is not my Work here to debate them; only since they are received and owned as such (for which we can, and

and have given our sufficient Reasons elsewhere, as for our other Principles) we ought to care how any, by walking otherwise, bring Reproach upon us; yet not to pass them wholly by. As to the First, Besides the Testimony of the Spirit of God in our Hearts (which is the original Ground of our Faith in all Things) we have the Testimony of the Apostle *Paul*, 2 *Cor.* 6. 14. *Be ye not unequally yoked together*, &c. Now if any should think, it were much from this Scripture to plead it absolutely unlawful, in any Case, to join in Marriage with any, (however otherwise sober) because of their not being one with us in all Things, I shall speak my Judgment. To me it appears so; and to many more who have obtained Mercy; *and we think we have the Spirit of God*. But whether it be lawful or not, I can say positively, *It is not expedient*, neither doth it edify, and (as that which is of dangerous Consequence) doth give justly Offence to the Church of Christ: And therefore no true tender Heart will prefer his private Love to the good and Interest of the whole Body.

As for the Second, In that we deny the Priests their assumed Authority and Power to marry, it is that which in no wise we can recede from, nor can we own any in the doing of it; it being a Part of our Testimony against the Usurpations of that Generation, who never yet, that I ever heard of, could produce any Scripture-proof, or Example for it.---- And seeing none can pretend Conscience in the Matter (for they themselves confess that it is no

<small>Test. 2. Against the Priests Usurpations.</small>

no Part of the Essence of Marriage) if any pretending to be among us, should, through Fear, Interest, or Prejudice to the Truth, come under, and bow to, that Image, have we not Reason to deny such slavish and ignoble Spirits, as mind not Truth and its Testimony?

Lastly, Seeing, if any walking with us, or going under the same Name, should *hastily* or *disorderly* go together, either being within the Degrees of Consanguinity, which the Law of God forbids, or that either Party should have been formerly under any Tie or Obligation to others, or any other vast Disproportion, which might bring a just Reflection upon us from our Opposers, can any blame us for taking Care to prevent these Evils, by appointing that such as so design, *make known their Intentions to these Churches or Assemblies, where they are most known,* that if any known just Cause of Hindrance, it may be mentioned, and a timous Lett put to the Hurt, either by stopping it, if they can be brought to *condescend;* or by refusing to be Witnesses and Concurrers with them in it, if they will not? For we take not upon us to hinder any to marry, otherwise than by Advice, or disconcerning ourselves; neither do we judge, that such as do *marry* contrary to our Mind, that therefore their Marriage is null and void in itself, or may be dissolved afterwards; Nay, all our meddling is in a holy Care for the Truth. For if the Thing be right, all that we do, is to be Witnesses; and if otherwise, that we may say for our Vindication

Sidenote: Test. 3. Against forbidden Degrees of Consanguinity and Pre-engagements. &c.

tion to such as may upbraid us therewith, that we *advised otherwise,* and did no Ways concur in the Matter; that so they may bear their own Burden, and the Truth and People of God be cleared.

Now I am confident that our Way herein is so answerable to Reason and Christianity, that none will blame us therefor; except either such, whose irregular and impatient Lusts cannot suffer a *serious and Christian Examination,* and an advised and moderate Procedure; or such, who watching for Evil against us, are sorry we should proceed so *Orderly,* and would rather we should suffer all Manner of Irregularities and Abominations, that they might have the more to say against us. But the solid and real Reasons we have for our Way herein, will sufficiently plead for us in the Hearts of all sober Men; and moreover, the Testimony of God's Spirit in our Hearts, doth abundantly confirm us both against the Folly of the one, and they Envy of the other.

<small>What Kind of Persons cannot bear the good Order of Truth.</small>

Fourthly, There being nothing more needful, than to *preserve Men and Women in Righteousness,* after they are brought into it; and also nothing more certain, than that the great Enemy of Man's Soul seeks daily how he may draw back again, and catch those who have in some Measure escaped his Snares, and known Deliverance from them; therefore do we also meet together, that we may receive an Opportunity to understand, if any have

<small>4. Our Care for restoring or separating Offenders.</small>

have fallen under his Temptations, that we may *restore* them again, if possible; or otherwise *separate* them from US. Surely, if we did not so, we might be justly blamed as such, among whom it were lawful to commit any Evil unreproved; indeed this were to be guilty of that *Libertinism* which some have falsely accused us of, and which hath been our Care all along, as became the People of God, to avoid: Therefore we have sought always to keep the House clean, by faithfully reproving and removing, according to the Nature of the Offence, and the Scandal following thereupon; private Things privately, and public Things publicly. We desire not to propagate Hurt, and defile Peoples Minds, with telling them such Things as tend not to edify; yet do we not so cover over, or smooth over any Wickedness, as not to deal roundly with the Persons guilty, and causing them to take away the Scandal in their Acknowledgment before all, to whose Knowledge it hath come: Yet judge we not ourselves obliged to *tell that in* Gath, *or publish that in the Streets of* Askelon, *which make the Daughters of the Uncircumcised rejoice;* or strengthen *Atheists* and *Ranters* in their Obdurateness, who feed more upon the Failings of the Saints, than to imitate their true Repentance. And therefore where we find an unfeigning Returning to the Lord, we desire not to remember that which the Lord hath forgotten; nor yet to throw Offences in the Way of the Weak, that they may stumble upon them.

And therefore I conclude, that our Care as to these Things also is most needful, and a Part of that

that *Order* and *Government*, which the Church of Chriſt never was, nor can be *without*; as doth abundantly appear by divers Scriptures heretofore mentioned.

Section VI.

How far this Government *doth extend in Matters* Spiritual, *and purely* Conſcientious.

THUS far I have conſidered the *Order* and Government of the Church, as it reſpects *outward Things*; and its Authority in condemning or removing ſuch Things, which in themſelves are Evil, as being thoſe, which none will readily juſtify: The Neceſſity of which Things is ſuch, that few but will acknowledge the Care and Order in theſe Caſes to be *commendable* and *expedient*.

Now I come to conſider the Things of another Kind, which either verily are, or are ſuppoſed to be Matters of CONSCIENCE, or at leaſt, wherein People may lay Claim to *Conſcience*, in the acting or forbearing of them. In which the great Queſtion is, *How far in ſuch Caſes the Church may give poſitive* Orders *or* Rules? *How far her Authority reacheth, or may be ſuppoſed to be binding, and ought to be ſubmitted to?* For the better clearing and Examination of which, it will be fit to conſider,

Firſt, *Whether the Church of Chriſt* Queſt. I. *hath Power in any Caſes that are Matters of Conſcience, to give a poſitive Sentence, and*

and *Decision*, which may be obligatory *upon Believers?*

Quest. II. Secondly, *If so, in what Cases and Respects she may so do?*

Quest. III. Thirdly, *Wherein consists the Freedom and Liberty of* Conscience, *which may be exercised by the Members of the true Church diversely, without judging one another?*

Quest. IV. And Lastly, *In whom the Power decisive is, in case of* Controversy, *or Contention in such Matters?*—Which will also lead us, *To observe the vast Difference betwixt* Us *and the* Papists, *and others in this Particular.*

Quest. I. As to the First, *Whether the Church of Christ hath Power in any Cases, that are Matters of* Conscience, *to give a positive Sentence and Decision, which may be obligatory upon Believers.*—

Answer. I answer affirmatively, *She hath*; and shall prove it from divers Instances, both from Scripture and Reason.

Articles of Faith are Matters of Conscience. For *First*, All *Principles* and *Articles* of *Faith*, which are held doctrinally, are, in respect to those that believe them, Matters of Conscience. We know the *Papists* do out of Conscience (such as are zealous among them) adore, worship and pray to *Angels, Saints* and *Images*, yea, and to the *Eucharist*, as judging it to be really Christ Jesus; and so do others place Conscience in Things that are absolutely wrong:

1. Proof from Right Reason. Now I say, we being gathered together into the Belief of certain Principles

ciples and Doctrines, without any Constraint or worldly Respect, but by the meer Force of Truth upon our Understanding, and its Power and Influence upon our Hearts; these Principles and Doctrines, and the Practices necessarily depending upon them, are, as it were, the *Terms* that have drawn us together, and the * *Bond*, by which we became centred into one *Body* and *Fellowship*, and distinguished from others. Now if any one, or more, so engaged with us, should arise to teach any other Doctrine or Doctrines, contrary to these which were the Ground of our being one; who can deny, but the Body hath Power in such a Case to declare, *This is not according to the Truth we profess; and therefore we pronounce such and such Doctrines to be wrong, with which we cannot have Unity, nor yet any more Spiritual-Fellowship with those that hold them?* And so cut themselves off from being Members, by dissolving the very Bond by which they were linked to the Body. Now this cannot be accounted *Tyranny* and *Oppression*, no more than in a civil Society, if one of the Society shall contradict one or more of the fundamental Articles, upon which the Society was contracted, it cannot be reckoned a Breach or Iniquity in the whole Society to declare, that such Contradictors

---

* *Yet this is not so the* Bond, *but* ⬛ *we have also a more inward and invisible, to wit, the* Life *of* Righteousness, *whereby we also have Unity with the upright Seed in all, even in those, whose Understandings are not yet so enlightened. But to those, who are once enlightened, this is as an* outward Bond; *and if they suffer themselves to be darkened through* Disobedience, *which as it does in the* outward Bond, *so it doth in the* inward.

tradictors have done wrong, and forfeited their Right in that Society; in case, by the original Constitution, the Nature of the Contradiction implies such a Forfeiture, as usually it is; and will no Doubt hold in religious Matters.

The Disbeliever of the Principles of a Fellowship excludes himself therefrom, and scatters.

As if a Body be gathered into one Fellowship, by the Belief, of certain Principles, he that comes to believe otherwise, naturally scattereth himself; for that the Cause, that gathered him, is taken away: And so those that abide constant in declaring the Thing to be so as it is, and in looking upon him, and witnessing of him to others (if need be) to be such, *as he has made himself*, do him no Injury. I shall make the Supposition in the General, and let every People make the Application to themselves, abstracting from us; and then let Conscience and Reason in every impartial Reader declare, whether or not it doth not hold? Suppose a People really gathered unto the Belief of the true and certain Principles of the Gospel, if any of these People shall arise and contradict any of those fundamental Truths, whether has not such as stand good Right to *cast such an one out* from among them, and to pronounce positively, *This is contrary to the Truth we profess and own; and therefore ought to be rejected, and not received, nor yet he that asserts it as one of us?* And is not this obligatory upon all the Members, seeing all are concerned in the like Care, as to themselves, to hold the Right and shut out the Wrong? I cannot tell, if any Man of Reason can well deny this: However, I shall

shall prove it next from the Testimony of the Scripture,

Gal. 1. 8. *But though we, or an Angel from Heaven, preach any other Gospel unto you, than that which we have preached unto you, let him be accursed. As we said before, so say I now again, if any Man preach any other Gospel unto you, than that ye have received, let him be accursed.* 1. Proof from Scripture.

1 Tim. 1. 19, 20. *Holding Faith and a good Conscience, which some having put away, concerning Faith, have made Shipwreck. Of whom is* Hymenæus *and* Alexander, *whom I have delivered unto Satan, that they may learn not to blaspheme.*

2 John 10. *If there come any unto you, and bring not this Doctrine, receive him not into your House, neither bid him rejoice.* (For so the *Greek* hath it.)

These Scriptures are so clear and plain in themselves, as to this Purpose, that they need no great Exposition to the unbiassed and unprejudicate Reader. For seeing it is so, that in the true Church there may Men arise, and speak perverse Things, contrary to the Doctrine and Gospel already received; what is to be the Place of those that hold the pure and ancient Truth? Must they look upon these perverse Men still as their Brethren? Must they cherish them as Fellow-Members, or must they judge, condemn and deny them? We must not think the Apostle wanted Charity, who will have them accursed; and that gave *Hymenæus* and *Alexander* over to Satan, after that they had departed from the true *Hymenæus* and *Alexander* instanced.

true Faith, that they might learn not to blaspheme. In short, if we must (as our Opposers herein acknowledge) preserve and keep those, that are come to own the Truth, by the same Means they were gathered and brought into it; we must not cease to be plain with them, and tell them, when they are wrong; and by sound Doctrine, both exhort and convince Gain-sayers. If the Apostles of Christ of old, and the Preachers of the everlasting Gospel in this Day, had told all People, however wrong they found them in their Faith and Principles, *Our Charity and Love is such, we dare not judge you, nor separate from you; but let us all live in Love together, and every one enjoy his own Opinion, and all will be well:* How should the Nations have been; or what Way can they be brought to *Truth* and *Righteousness?* Would not the *Devil love* this *Doctrine* well, by which *Darkness* and *Ignorance,* Error and Confusion might still continue in the Earth unreproved, and uncondemned? If it was needful then for the Apostles of Christ in the Days of old to reprove, without sparing to tell the High-Priests, and great Professors among the *Jews, that they were stubborn and stiff-necked, and always resisted the Holy Ghost,* without being guilty of Imposition and Oppression, or Want of true Love and Charity; and also for those Messengers the Lord raised up in this Day, to reprove and cry out against the Hireling-Priests, and to tell the World openly, both Professors and Prophane, *that they were in Darkness and Ignorance, out of the Truth,*

Strangers

<small>A wrong Charity and false Love to cherish in Error—is—</small>

Strangers and Aliens from the Common-Wealth of Israel; if God has gathered a People, by this Means, into the Belief of one and the same Truth, must not they, if they turn and depart from it, be admonished, reproved and condemned, (yea, rather than those that are not yet come to the Truth) because they crucify afresh unto themselves the Lord of Glory, and put him to open Shame? It seems the Apostle judged it very needful they should be so dealt with, *Tit.* 1. 10. when he says, *There are many unruly and vain Talkers and Deceivers, especially they of the Circumcision*, WHOSE MOUTHS MUST BE STOPPED, &c. Were such a Principle to be received or believed, that in the Church of Christ no Man should be separated from, no Man condemned or excluded the Fellowship and Communion of the Body, for his Judgment or Opinion in Matters of Faith, then what Blasphemies so horrid, what Heresies so damnable, what Doctrines of Devils, but might harbour itself in the Church of Christ? What Need then of sound Doctrine, if no Doctrine make unsound? What Need of convincing and exhorting Gain-sayers, if to gain-say be no Crime? Where should the Unity of the Faith be? Were not this an Inlet to all Manner of Abomination; and to make void the whole Tendency of Christ, and his Apostles Doctrine; and render the Gospel of none Effect; and give a Liberty to the unconstant and giddy Will of Man to innovate, alter and overturn it at his Pleasure? So that from all that is above mentioned,

---The Inlet of all Manner of Abominations.

we

we do safely conclude, that where a People are gathered together into the Belief of the Principles and Doctrines of the Gospel of Christ, if any of that People shall go from their Principles, and assert Things false and contrary to what they have already received; such as stand and abide firm in the Faith, have Power, by the Spirit of God, after they have used Christian Endeavours to convince and reclaim them, upon their Obstinacy to separate from such, and to exclude them from their spiritual Fellowship and Communion: For otherwise, if this be denied, farewel to all Christianity, or to the maintaining of any sound Doctrine in the Church of Christ.

Quest. 2. But, *Secondly*, Taking it for granted, that the Church of Christ, or Assembly of Believers, may, in some Cases, that are Matter of Conscience, pronounce a positive *Sentence* and *Judgment* without Hazard of Imposition upon the Members, it comes to be enquired; *In what Cases, and how far this Power reacheth?*

Answer. I Answer, *First*, As that which is most clear and undeniable, in the fundamental Principles and Doctrines of Faith, in case any should offer to teach otherwise, as is above declared and proved. But some may perhaps acknowledge that indeed if any should contradict the known and owned Principles of Truth, and teach otherwise, it were fit to cast out and exclude such; but what judgest thou as to lesser Matters, as in Principles of less Consequence, or in *outward* Ceremonies or Gestures, whether it be fit to press Uniformity in these Things? For Answer to this, it is fit to consider, *First*,

First, *The Nature of the Things themselves.* — Confideration 1.

Secondly, *The Spirit and Ground they proceed from.* — 2.

And Thirdly, *The Consequence and Tendency of them.* — 3.

But before I proceed upon these, I affirm, and that according to Truth, that as the Church and Assembly of God's People may, and hath Power to decide by the Spirit of God in Matters fundamental and weighty, (without which no Decision nor Decree in whatever Matters is available;) so the same Church and Assembly also, in other Matters of less Moment, as to themselves, (yet being needful and expedient with a Respect to the *Circumstance* of Time, Place and other Things that may fall in,) may and hath Power by the same Spirit, and not otherwise, being acted, moved and assisted, and led by it thereto, to pronounce a positive Judgment: Which, no Doubt, will be found obligatory upon all such who have a Sense and Feeling of the Mind of the Spirit, though rejected by such as are not watchful, and so are out of the Feeling and Unity of the Life. And this is that which none that own immediate Revelation, or a being inwardly led by the Spirit, to be now a Thing expected or dispensed to the Saints, can, without contradicting their own Principle, deny; far less such with whom I have to do in this Matter, who claiming this Privilege to Particulars, saying, *That they being moved to do such and such Things, though contrary to the Mind and Sense*

The Decision of Matters of less Moment in the Church obligatory.

of

of their Brethren, are not to be judged for it; adding, *Why may it not be so, that God hath moved them to it?* Now if this be a sufficient Reason for them to suppose as to *one* or *two*, I may without Absurdity suppose it as well to the whole Body. And therefore as to the First, to wit,

Conf. 1.

Against the Reproach of Truth.

The Nature of the Things themselves. If it be such a Thing, the doing or not doing whereof, that is, either any Act, or the Forbearance of any, may bring a real Reproach or Ground of Accusation against the Truth professed and owned, and in and through which there may a visible Schism and Dissention arise in the Church, by which Truth's Enemies may be gratified, and itself brought into Disesteem; then it is fit for such, whose Care is to keep all right, to take Inspection in the Matter, to meet together in the Fear of God, to wait for his Counsel, and to speak forth his Mind, according as he shall manifest himself in and among them. And this was the Practice of the primitive Church in the Matter of *Circumcision*. For here lay the Debate: Some thought it not needful to circumcise the *Gentiles*; others thought it a Thing not to be dispensed with: And no Doubt, of these, (for we must remember, they were not the rebellious *Jews*, but such as had already believed in Christ) there were that did it out of Conscience, as judging Circumcision to be still obligatory. For they said thus, *except ye be circumcised after the Manner of* Moses, *ye cannot be saved.* Now what Course took the Church of *Antioch* in these Cases? *Acts* 15. 2.

They

They determined that Paul *and* Barnabas, *and certain other of them should go unto* Jerusalem, *unto the Apostles and Elders, about this Question.* We must not suppose they wanted the Spirit of God at *Antioch* to have decided the Matter, neither that these Apostles neglected or went from their inward Guide in undertaking this Journey; yet we see, they judged it meet in this Matter to have the Advice and Concurrence of the Apostles and Elders, that were at *Jerusalem*, that they might be all of one Mind in the Matter. For there is no greater Property of the Church of Christ, than pure Unity in the Spirit; that is, a consenting and Oneness in Judgment, and Practice in Matters of Faith and Worship (which yet admits of different Measures, Growths and Motions, but never contrary and contradictory Ones; and in these Diversities of Operations, yet still, by the same Spirit, the true Liberty is exercised, as shall be declared hereafter;) Therefore prayeth Christ, *That they all may be One, as he and the Father is One.* To which Purpose also let these following Scriptures be examined:

The Church at Antioch sends a Case to Jerusalem for Advice from the Elders.

Rom. 12. 16. *Be of the same Mind one towards another.*

1 Cor. 1. 10. *Now I beseech you, Brethren, by the Name of our Lord Jesus Christ, that ye all speak the same Thing, and that there be no Divisions among you; but that ye be perfectly joined together in the same Mind, and in the same Judmgent.*

Ephes. 5. 21. *Submitting yourselves one to another in the Fear of God.*

Phil.

Phil. 2. 2. *Fulfil ye my Joy, that ye be like-minded, having the same Love, being of one Accord, of one Mind.*

And yet more remarkable is that of the Apostle *Paul* to the *Philippians*, Chap. 3. Verse 15. *Let us therefore, as many as be perfect, be thus minded; and if in any Thing ye be otherwise minded, God shall reveal even this unto you.*

Verse 16. *Nevertheless, whereto we have already attained, let us walk by the same Rule, let us mind the same Thing.*

Verse 17. *Brethren, be Followers together of me, and mark them which walk so, as ye have us for an Example.*

<small>Pretenders and Innovators judged by the Power of God.</small> So here, though the Apostle grants Forbearance in Things whereto they have not yet attained; yet he concludes they must walk so, as they have him for an Example, and so consequently not contrary, or otherwise. And therefore we conclude that whereas any in the Church of God pretending *Conscience* or *Revelation*, shall arise to teach and practise (however insignificant or small in themselves) whether Principles or Practices, yet if they be contrary to such as are already received as true, and confirmed by God's Spirit in the Hearts of the Saints, and that the introducing of these Things tend to bring Reproach upon the Truth, as such as are not edifying in themselves, and so stumble the Weak; those who have a true and right Discerning, may, in and by the Power of God authorizing them (and no otherwise) *condemn* and *judge* such Things: And they so doing it, it will be obligatory

gatory upon all the Members that have a true Senfe, becaufe they will feel it to be fo, and therefore fubmit to it. And thus far as to the Nature of the Things themfelves.

Secondly, As *to the Spirit and Ground they proceed from.* Whatfoever Innovation, Difference, or divers Appearance, whether in Doctrine or Practice, proceedeth not from the pure Moving of the Spirit of God, or is not done out of pure Tendernefs of Confcience, but either from that, which being puft up, affecteth Singularity, and therethrough would be obferved, commended and exalted; or from that, which is the Malignity of fome Humours and natural Tempers, which will be contradicting without Caufe, and fecretly begetting of Divifions, Animofities and Emulations, by which the Unity and unfeigned Love of the Brethren is leffened or rent; I fay, all Things proceeding from this Root and Spirit, however little they may be fuppofed to be of themfelves, are to be guarded againft, withftood and denied, as hurtful to the true Church's Peace, and a Hindrance to the Profperity of Truth. *Conf. 2.* What proceeds not from the Spirit of God, to be withftood and denied.

If it be faid, *How know ye that thefe Things proceed from that Ground?* Queftion.

For Anfwer, I make not here any Application, as to particular Perfons or Things; but if it be granted (as it cannot be denied, that there may arife Perfons in the true Church, that may do fuch Things from such Anfwer.

such a Spirit, though pretending *Conscience* and *Tenderness*; then it must also be acknowledged, that such, to whom God hath given a true Discerning by his Spirit, may and ought to judge such Practices, and the Spirit they come from, and have no Unity with them, which if it be owned in the general, proves the Case, to wit, That some pretending Conscience in Things seeming indifferent, but yet it proceeding in them from a Spirit of *Singularity, Emulation,* or *Strife*, those that have received a Discerning thereof from the Lord, may and ought to judge the Transgressors, without being accounted *Imposers, Oppressors of Conscience,* or *Inforcers of Uniformity*, contrary to the Mind of Christ; against which the Apostle also guardeth the Churches of old.

The Spirit of discerning in the Church, judges Transgressors.

Phil. 2. 3, 4. *Let nothing be done through Strife, or vain Glory; but in Lowliness of Mind let each esteem other* BETTER THAN THEMSELVES.

Look not every Man on his own Things; but every Man also on the Things of others.

Now, if it be an Evil to do any Thing out of Strife; then such Things that are seen so to be done, are they not to be avoided and forsaken? So that we are confident, our Judgment herein cannot be denied, or reputed erroneous; except it be said, *That none will or can arise in the Church of Christ, pretending such Things from such a Spirit*; which I know not any that will, it being contrary to the express

Pretenders may arise, and must be watched against.

express Prophesies of the Scripture, and the Experience of the Church in all Ages, as may appear from *Mat.* 24. 24. *Acts* 15. 24. 1 *Tim.* 4. 1. 2 *Tim.* 3. 8. *Mark* 13. 21, 22. 2 *Pet.* 2. 19. Or on the other Hand, that those that abide faithful, and have a Discerning of those Evils, ought to be silent, and never ought to reprove and gain-stand them, nor yet warn and guard others against them; and that it is a Part of the commendable Unity of the Church of Christ, to suffer all such Things without taking Notice of them. I know none will say so; but if there be any so foolish as to affirm it, let them consider these Scriptures, *Gal.* 2. 4. 1 *Tim.* 1. 20. 2 *Tim.* 2. 24, 25. *Tit.* 1. 9, 10, 11.

<small>Discerners of Evils to reprove and warn.</small>

Now if none of these hold true; but, on the contrary, such Evils have been, and may be found to creep in among the People of God, and that such as see them, may and ought to reprove them; then necessarily the doing so, is neither Imposition, Force nor Oppression.

As to the *Third, concerning the Consequence and Tendency of them,* it is mostly included in the two former: For whatsoever tendeth not to Edification, but, on the contrary, to Destruction, and to beget Discord among Brethren, is to be avoided: According to that of the Apostle, *Rom.* 16. 17. *Now I beseech you, Brethren, mark them which cause Divisions and Offences, contrary to the Doctrine which ye have learned, and avoid them.*

<small>Conf. 3. --Sowers of Discord among Brethren to be avoided.</small>

And

And since there is no greater Mark of the People of God, than to be at Peace among themselves; whatsoever tendeth to break that Bond of Love and Peace, must be testified against. Let it be observed, I speak always of the Church of Christ *indeed*, and deal with such as are of another Mind; not as reckoning only false Churches not to have this Power, but denying it even to the true Church of Christ, as judging it not fit for her so to act, as in Relation to her Members. For though Christ be the *Prince of Peace*, and doth most of all commend Love and Unity to his Disciples; yet I also know he came not to send Peace, but a Sword, that is, in dividing Man from the Lusts and Sins he hath been united to.

—To follow Peace among ourselves—

And also it is the Work of his Disciples and Messengers, to break the Bands and Unity of the Wicked, wherein they are banded against God, and his Truth, and the Confederacy of such as stand in Unrighteousness, by inviting and bringing as many as will obey, unto Righteousness; whereby they become disunited and separated from their Companions, with whom they were centred, and at Peace, in the contrary and cursed Nature. And indeed, blessed are they that are sent forth of the Lord to scatter here, that they may gather into the Unity of the Life: And they are blessed that, in this Respect, even for Righteousness Sake, are scattered and separated from their Brethren; that they may come to know the Brother-hood and Fellowship which is

—To the breaking of the Bands of the Wicked.

Prov. 20. 26.

in the Light; from which none ought to scatter, nor be scattered, but the more and more gathered thereunto. And this leads me to what I proposed in the *third Place*, under this Head, of the *true Churches Power in Matters Spiritual*, or *purely Conscientious*; which may be thus objected:

If thou plead so much for an One-   Quest. 3.
ness *in the* smallest Matters, *wherein consisteth the Freedom and Liberty of the Conscience, which may be exercised by the Members of the true Church diversely, without judging one another?*

In Answer to this Proposition, I   Answer.
affirm, first in general, that whatsoever Things may be supposed to proceed from the same Spirit, though diverse in its appearance, tending to the same End of Edification, and which in the Tendency of it, layeth not a real Ground for Division, or Dissension of Spirit, Fellow-Members ought not only to bear one another, but strengthen one another in them.

Now the Respects wherein this may be, I can describe no better than the Apostle *Paul* doth principally in two Places, which therefore will be fit to consider at Length for the Opening of this Matter; this being one of the weightiest Points pertaining to this Subject. Because, as on the one Hand due Forbearance ought to be exercised in its right Place; so on the other, the many Devices and false Pretences of the Enemy creeping in here, ought to be guarded against.

The first is, 1 *Cor.* 12. from Verse   Place 1.
4. to 31. thus:

M   Verse

Diversities of Gifts, Administrations and Operations from the same Spirit makes no Division.

Verse 4. *Now there are Diversities of Gifts, but the same Spirit.*

Verse. 5. *And there are Differences of Administrations, but the same Lord.*

Verse 6. *And there are Diversities of Operations, but it is the same God which worketh all in all.*

Verse 7. *But the Manifestation of the Spirit is given to every Man to profit withal.*

Verse 8. *For to one is given by the Spirit the Word of Wisdom, to another the Word of Knowledge by the same Spirit.*

Verse 9. *To another Faith by the same Spirit, to another the Gifts of Healing by the same Spirit.*

Verse 10. *To another the Working of Miracles, to another Prophecy, to another Discerning of Spirits, to another divers Kinds of Tongues, to another the Interpretation of Tongues.*

Verse 11. *But all these worketh that one and the self-same Spirit, dividing to every Man severally, as he will.*

As many Members in one Body concur to the upholding the same.

Verse 12. *For as the Body is One, and hath many Members, and all the Members of that one Body being many, are one Body, so also is Christ.*

Verse 13. *For by one Spirit are we all baptised into one Body, whether we be* Jews *or* Gentiles, *whether we be bond or free; and have been all made to drink into one Spirit.*

Verse 14. *For the Body is not one Member, but many.*

Verse

Verse 15. *If the Foot shall say, because I am not the Hand, I am not of the Body; is it therefore not of the Body?*

Verse 16. *And if the Ear shall say, because I am not the Eye, I am not of the Body; is it therefore not of the Body?*

Verse 17. *If the whole Body were an Eye, where were the Hearing? If the whole were Hearing, where were the Smelling?*

Verse 18. *But now hath God set the Members every one of them in the Body, as it hath pleased Him.*

Verse 19. *And if they were all one Member, where were the Body?*

Verse 20. *But now are they many Members, yet but one Body.*

Verse 21. *And the Eye cannot say unto the Hand, I have no Need of thee; nor again, the Head to the Feet, I have no Need of you?*

Verse 22. *Nay, much more those Members of the Body, which seem to be more feeble, are necessary.*

Verse 23. *And those Members of the Body, which we think to be less honourable, upon these we bestow more abundant Honour, and our uncomely Parts have more abundant Comeliness.*

Verse 24. *For our comely Parts have no Need, but God hath tempered the Body together, having given more abundant Honour to that Part which lacked:*

Verse 25. *That there should be no Schism in the Body; but that the Members should have the same Care one of another.*

Verse 26. *And whether one Member suffer, all the Members suffer with it; or one Member be honoured, all the Members rejoice with it.*

Verse 27. *Now ye are the Body of Christ, and Members in particular:*

Verse 28. *And God hath set some in the Church, first Apostles, secondarily Prophets, thirdly Teachers, after that Miracles, then Gifts of Healing, Helps, Governments, Diversities of Tongues.*

Verse 29. *Are all Apostles? Are all Prophets? Are all Teachers? Are all Workers of Miracles?*

Verse 30. *Have all the Gifts of Healing? Do all speak with Tongues? Do all interpret?*

Which I would not have set down at large, but that there be some so careless (especially in Matters they like not) that they will scarce be at the Pains seriously to read over a Citation only named; and that also this being presented before the Reader, in the Current of the Discourse, will fix the Nature of my Application the more in his Understanding. For the Apostle shews here the Variety of the Operations of the divers Members of the Body of Christ, working to one and the same End; as the divers Members of a Man's Body towards the maintaining and upholding of the Whole.

<small>The Sum of the Premises.</small>

Now these are not placed in contrary Workings, for so they would destroy one another; and so the Apostle in the ordering of them in three several Kinds proves this. First, *Diversities of Gifts.* Secondly, *Differences of Administrations.* Thirdly, *Diversities of Operations*: And that which is the Bond that keeps the Oneness, here he also mentions, to wit, *The same Spirit, the same Lord, the same God;* The Apostle names nothing of Contrariety or Opposition. But lest any should

should be so critical, as to bring in here the School-Distinction of *Contrarium Oppositum*, and *Contradictorium*, I shall not deny, but *Contrariety* or *Opposition*, in the Sense it is sometimes taken, may be found in the Body without *Schism*: As the *comely Parts* may be said to be *opposite* or *contrary* to the *Uncomely*, or the *Left-hand* contrary to the *Right*, or the *Foot* opposite to the *Head*, as the uppermost Part to the undermost; or the *doing* a Thing is contrary to the *forbearing* of it; but as for that which is acknowledged to be *Propositions*, or *Termini contradictorii*, that is, *contradictory Propositions*, which are in themselves irreconcileable, whereof one must be still wrong, and that still destroy one another, and work contrary Effects, they are not at all admitted, nor supposed to be in the Body of Christ; as I shall give in one Instance, Verse 8. *To one is given by the Spirit the Word of Wisdom, to another the Word of Knowledge, by the same Spirit.* First, here are *two different Gifts*, but not *contrary*. Secondly, There may something like Contrariety, in the Sense aforementioned, be here supposed; as some may want this Gift of *Wisdom* and *Knowledge*, and so *to have* is contrary *to want*; (though as to these two, none may be absolutely said to want them; yet all have them not in the same Degree, as a *special Gift*; though as to some Gifts there may be an absolute Want, as that of *Miracles*, and *Interpretation of Tongues*.) But should I suppose such a Contrariety, or more properly a *Contradiction*, as to

No Contrariety in the Body of Christ.

Instances.
1.
2.

to *Wisdom*, to oppose *Folly*, and to *Knowledge*, utter *Ignorance*; this were an Opposition not to be admitted of in the Body, because it were false to suppose that to proceed from the same Spirit. And *such Contrarieties* or *Diversities*, as cannot justly be supposed to proceed from the same Spirit of God, which is the Bond that links together, cannot be mutually entertained in the Body; so the *Differences* and *Diversities*, which the Apostle admits of, while he speaks largely in this Matter, are, *That none ought to be offended at his Brother, that he hath not the same Work and Office in the Body that he hath; but that every one keep in his own Place, as God hath appointed them; that neither them that are set in a higher Place, despise them that are set in a lower; nor them that are set in a lower, grudge and repine at such as are set higher; but all work in their proper Place, towards the Edification of the Whole.* And that the Apostle intends this, is manifest, where he draws to a Conclusion, Verse 27. *Now ye are the Body of Christ, and Members in particular, and God hath set some in the Church, first Apostles, secondly Prophets,* &c. and then he subsumes, *Are all Apostles,* &c.

<small>Diversities of Works and Operations in the Body.</small>

<small>Place 2.</small> Which the same *Paul* again confirms, *Ephes.* 4. 8, 11. to the 17th, which was the second Place I intended; and shall only mention, for Brevity's Sake, leaving the Reader to consider of it at his Leisure.

This is also held forth by the beloved Disciple *John*, in his threefold Distinction, 1 *John* 2. 12, 13.

Of Fathers, young Men, and *little Children:* And by *Peter,* 1 *Pet.* 5. 1, 5. in that of *Elders* and *Younger.* The true Liberty then in the Church of Christ is exercised when as one judgeth not another in these different Places; but live in Love together, all minding the Unity and general Good of the Body, and to work their own Work in their own Place. Also the Forbearance of the Saints is exercised, when as they judge not one another for being found in the different Appearance, either of *doing* or *forbearing*; which may be peculiar to their several Places and Stations in the Body: For that there is, and may be Diversities of Works there, is excellently well expressed by the Apostles, *viz.*

[sidenote: The true Liberty in the Church.]

[sidenote: Diversities of Works expressed by the Apostles.]

Rom. 12. 3. *For I say through the Grace given unto me, to every Man that is among you, not to think of himself more highly than he ought to think; but to think soberly according as God hath dealt to every Man the Measure of Faith.*

Verse 4. *For as we have many Members in one Body, and all Members have not the same Office:*

Verse 5. *So we being many, are one Body in Christ, and every one Members one of another.*

Verse 6. *Having then Gifts differing, according to the Grace that is given to us, whether Prophecy, let us prophesy according to the Proportion of Faith.*

Verse 7. *Or Ministry, let us wait on our Ministring; or he that teacheth, on Teaching:*

Verse 8. *Or he that exhorteth, on Exhortation: He that giveth let him do it with Simplicity; he that*

that ruleth with Diligence; he that sheweth Mercy with Chearfulness.

If any then should quarrel with his Brother, for exercising that which belongeth to the Office of the Body Christ hath called him to, and would force him to exercise the same Office he doth, though he be not called to it; here is a Breach of Christian Liberty, and an imposing upon it.

The Breach of Liberty begets Jarrs and Schisms.

Now all Schisms and Jarrs fall out in this two-fold Respect: Either when any Person or Persons assume another, or an higher Place in the Body, than God will have them to be in, and so exercise an Office, or go about to perform that, which they ought not to do; or when, as any truly exercising in their Place, which God hath given them, others rise up and judge them, and would draw them from it; both of which Cases have been, and may be supposed to fall out in the Church of Christ: As 1 *Cor.* 4. 3, 4. where some judged *Paul* wrongously; 3 *John* 9. where one exalting himself above his Place, judged whom he ought not. We see then what Diversities be most usually in the Church of God, consisting in the Difference of the Gift proceeding from the same Spirit; and in the divers Places, that the several Members have in the same Body for the Edification of it; and every one being here in his own Station, his standing therein is his Strength and Perfection; and to be in another, though higher and more eminent, would but weaken and hurt him: And so in this there ought to be a mutual Forbearance, that there may neither be a coveting nor aspiring on the one Hand, nor yet a despising or condemning
on

on the other. But besides the Forbearance of this Nature, which is most ordinary and universal (and for the Exercise whereof there is, and will still be a Need, so long as there is any Gathering or Church of Christ upon the Earth) there is a certain Liberty and Forbearance also, that is more particular, and has a Relation to the Circumstance of Times and Places, which will not hold universally; whereof we have the Example of the primitive Church, testified by the Scriptures in two or three Particulars. The first was, *In suffering Circumcision to the* Jews *for a Time*, and not only so, but also divers others of the legal and ceremonial Purifications and Customs, as may appear, *Acts* 21. Ver. 21, 22, 23, 24, &c. The second was, *In the Observation of certain Days, Rom.* 14. 5. And the third, *In the abstaining from Meats*, 1 *Cor*. 8. throughout: Here the Apostle perswades to, and recommends a Forbearance, because of the Weakness of some; for he says not any where, nor can it be found in all the Scriptures of the Gospel, that these Things such weak Ones were exercised in, were Things indispensably necessary, or that it had been better for them they had not been under such Scruples, providing it had been from a Principle of true Clearness, and so of Faith.

Acts of Forbearance in the primitive Church.

Next again, These Acts of Forbearance were done in a Condescension to the Weakness of such, upon whom the antient (and truly deserved in its Season) Veneration of the Law had such a deep Impression, that they

Acts of Forbearance or Condescension under the Law.

they could not yet dispense with all its Ceremonies and Customs: And to such the Apostle holds forth a two-fold Forbearance.

First, A certain Compliance by such Believers, as were gathered out from the *Jews*; though they saw over these Things, yet it was fit they should condescend somewhat to their Countrymen and Brethren, who were weak.

1. To *Jews*.

Secondly, the like Forbearance in the *Gentiles*, not to judge them in these Things; but we see, that it was not allowed for such weak Ones to propagate these Scruples, or draw others into them; and that when as any of the Churches of the *Gentiles*, who wanted this Occasion, would have been exercising this Liberty, or pleading for it, the Apostle doth down-rightly condemn it, as I shall make appear in all the three Instances above mentioned.

2. To Gentiles.

First, In that of *Circumcision*, *Gal.* 5. 2, 4.

1. Of Circumcision.

Behold, I Paul *say unto you, that if ye be circumcised, Christ shall profit you nothing; Christ is become of none Effect unto you: Whosoever of you are justified by the Law, ye are fallen from Grace.*

Can there be any Thing more positive? Might not some here have pretended Tenderness of Conscience, and have said, *Though the Decree of the Apostles do dispense with Circumcision in me; yet if I find a Scruple in myself, and a Desire to it out of Tenderness, why should it be an Evil in me to do it, more than in the* Jews *that believe?* We see,

see, there is no Room left here for such Reasoning.

Secondly, As to *Observations*, *Gal.* 4. 9, 10, 11. Might not they have answered, *What if we regard a Day to the Lord, must we not then? Are not these thy own Words?* We see that did not hold here, because in them it was a *Returning to the beggarly Elements*. Inst. 2. of Observations of Days.

Thirdly, As to *Meats*, 1 *Tim.* 4. 3. Here we see that is accounted a Doctrine of Devils; which in another Respect was *Christian Forbearance*. And therefore now, and that in the general Respect, he gives this Reason, Verse 4. *For every Creature of God is good, and nothing to be refused, if it be received with Thanksgiving of them that believe, and know the Truth.* So we see, that in these particular Things there is great Need of Wariness in the Church of Christ; for that sometimes *Forbearance* under a Pretence of Liberty may be more hurtful than down-right *Judging*. I suppose, if any should arise, and pretend Conscience, and claim a Liberty for *Circumcision*, and the *Purifications of the Law*, whether all Christians would not with one Voice condemn it? And so as to *Days* and *Meats*, how do the Generality of *Protestants* judge it? Though I deny not but there may, and ought to be a mutual Forbearance in the Church of Christ in certain such Cases, which may fall in; and a Liberty there is in the Lord, which breaks not the Peace of the true Church; but in such Matters (as I observed at large before) both the Nature of the Things, the Spirit

Spirit they come from, and the Occasion from whence, and their Consequence and Tendency is to be carefully observed.

Section VII.

Concerning the Power of Decision.

SEeing, then, it may fall out in the Church of Christ, that both some may assume another Place in the Body than they ought, and others may lay Claim to a Liberty, and pretend Conscience in Things they ought not, and that without Question the Wrong is not to be tolerated, but to be testified against, however specious its Appearance may be; and that it must, and ought to be judged: The Question will arise, *Who is the proper Judge or Judges, in whom resideth the Power of deciding this Controversy?* And this is that which I undertook, in the next Place, to treat of, as being the specifick Difference, and distinguishing Property of the Church of Christ, from all other antichristian Assemblies and Churches of Man's building and framing.

<small>Head III. Proposition 2.</small>

To give a short, and yet clear and plain Answer to this Proposition: *The only proper Judge of Controversies in the Church, is the Spirit of God, and the Power of deciding solely lies in it; as having the only unerring, infallible and certain Judgment belonging to it; which Infallibility is not necessarily annexed to any Persons, Person or Places whatsoever, by Virtue of*

<small>The Spirit of God the proper Judge of Controversies in the Church.</small>

of any Office, Place or Station any one may have, or have had in the Body of Chrift. That is to fay, that any have Ground to reafon thus, *Becaufe I am, or have been fuch an eminent Member, therefore my Judgment is infallible*; or, *Becaufe we are the greateft Number*; or, that *we live in fuch a noted or famous Place*, or the like: Though fome of thefe Reafons may, and ought to have their true Weight in Cafes of *contradictory* Affertions (as fhall hereafter be obferved) yet not fo, as upon which either mainly, or only the infallible Judgment is to be placed; but upon the Spirit, as that which is the firm and unmoveable Foundation.

And now, if I fhould go on no further, I have faid enough to vindicate us from *IMPOSITION*, and from the Tyranny, whether of *Popery, Prelacy*, or *Prefbytery*, or any fuch like we have, been or may be branded with, as fhall after appear.

But to proceed: Herein lies the Difference betwixt the Difpenfation of the Law, and the Gofpel or New-Covenant; for that of old all Anfwers were to be received from the Priefts in the Tabernacle. For he, that appeared betwixt the Cherubims there, fpake forth his Mind to the People; and there were alfo Families of the Prophets, to whom they reforted for the Anfwer of the Lord (though fometimes, as a Signification of the further Glory that was to be revealed, it pleafed God to reveal his Mind to fome, even to them, who were neither Prophets nor Prophets Sons) but, under the Gofpel, we are all to be taught of God, that is, none are excluded from

Exod. 25. 22.
Numb. 7. 89.
Hof. 12. 10.
Amos 7. 14.
2 Chron. 18. 6, 7. John 6. 45. Heb. 1. 1, 2.

from this Privilege, by not being of
Levi, or of the Children of the Prophe
this Privilege is as truly exercised
aſſenting and obeying to what God
and reveals through others (they fe
with it in the Life) as by ſuch, who
velation and Command of God's Spir
his Will to his People in certain Partic
the ſame Spirit leads and comman
obey. So that we ſay, and that
good Ground, that it is no Way inco
this ſound and unerrir

<small>Judgment in-
fallible pro-
ceeds from
the Spirit in-
fallible.</small>
to affirm, That the Jud
certain Perſon or Perſon
Caſes is infallible, or f
Perſon or Perſons to gi
Judgment, and pronoun

ligatory upon others, becauſe the Fou
Ground thereof is, not becauſe they a
but becauſe in theſe Things, and a
they were led by the infallible
therefore it will not ſhelter any in
to pretend, *I am not bound to obey th
fallible Man; is not this* Popery, *I no
ſwaded in myſelf?* Becauſe it is not
dient to them, but to the Judgmer
through them at ſuch a Time; and c
their not being perſwaded, may as p
ceed from their being hardned, and
of their Place, and in an Incapacity
Requirings, as that the Thing is not
them, which none can deny; but it
be ſuppoſed, as the contrary. But
ther clearing of this Matter, before

I shall not doubt both to affirm and prove these following *Propositions*.

First, That there never will, nor can be wanting, in case of Controversy, the Spirit of God, to give Judgment through some or other in the Church of Christ, so long as any Assembly can properly, or in any tolerable Supposition be so termed. <small>Assert. 1.</small>

Secondly, That God hath ordinarily, in the communicating of his Will under his Gospel, employed such whom he had made Use of in gathering of his Church, and in feeding and watching over them; though not excluding others. <small>Assert. 2.</small>

Thirdly, That their *de Facto*, or effectual Meeting together, and giving a positive Judgment in such Cases, will not import *Tyranny* and *Usurpation*, or an Inconsistency with the universal Privilege that all Christians have to be led by the Spirit; neither will the Pretences of any contradicting them, or refusing to submit upon the Account they see it not, or so, excuse them from being really guilty of disobeying God. <small>Assert. 3.</small>

For the *First*, to those that believe the Scripture, there will need no other Probation than that of *Matt.* 28. 20. *And lo, I am with you alway, even unto the End of the World.* And Verse 18. *And the Gates of Hell shall not prevail against it.* <small>Assert. 1. Proved.</small>

Now if the Church of Christ were so destitute of the Spirit of God, that in case of Difference there were not any found that, by the infallible Spirit, could give a certain Judgment; would not then the Gates <small>The infallible Spirit the Gates of Hell cannot prevail against.</small>

of

of Hell prevail againſt it? For where Strife and Diviſion is, and no effectual Way to put an End to it, there not only the Gates, but the Courts and inner Chambers of Darkneſs prevail; for where Envy and Strife is, there is Confuſion and every evil Work.

But that there may be here no Ground of Miſtake or Suppoſition, that we were annexing *Infallibility* to certain Perſons, or limiting the Church to ſuch; I underſtand not by the Church, every particular Gathering or Aſſembly, circumſcribed to any particular Country or City: For I will not refuſe but divers of them, both apart and together, if not eſtabliſhed in God's Power, may err. Nor yet do I lay the abſolute Streſs upon a general Aſſembly of Perſons, as ſuch, picked and choſen out of every one of thoſe particular Churches; as if what the Generality or Plurality of thoſe conclude upon, were neceſſarily to be ſuppoſed to be the infallible Judgment of Truth: Though to ſuch an Aſſembly of Perſons truly ſtated (as they ought) in God's Power, he hath heretofore revealed his Will in ſuch Caſes; and yet may as the moſt probable Way; (which ſhall be ſpoken of hereafter:) Yet ſuch as a meer Aſſembly, is not concluſive, nor yet do I underſtand by the Church, every Gathering or Aſſembly of People, who may hold found and true Principles, or have a Form of Truth; for ſome may loſe the Life and Power of Godlineſs, who notwithſtanding may retain the Form or Notions of Things, but yet are to be *turned away from*, becauſe in

The erring Church or People.--

---Having the Form of Truth.

ſo

so far (as I observed before) as Sanctification, to wit, those that are sanctified in Christ Jesus, make the Church, and give the right Definition to it: Where that is wholly wanting, the Church of Christ ceaseth to be; and there remains nothing but a Shadow without Substance. Such Assemblies then are like the dead Body, when the Soul is departed, which is no more fit to be conversed with; because it corrupts, and proves noisome to the Living. But by the Church of Christ, I understand all those that truly and really have received and hold the Truth, as it is in Jesus, and are in Measure sanctified, or sanctifying in and by the Power and Virtue thereof working in their inward Parts; and this may be made up of divers distinct *Gatherings* or Churches in several Countries or Nations: I say, so long as these, or any of them retain that, which justly entitles them the Church or Churches of Christ. (which they may be truly called) though there may fall out some Differences, Divisions or Schisms among them; as we may see there was no small Dissention in the Church of *Antioch*, and yet it ceased not to be a Church, *Acts* 15. 2. and 1 *Cor.* 1. 11.

The true Church.

For it hath been declared unto me of you, my Brethren, that there are Contentions among you; and yet, Verse 2. he entitles them the Church of God, them that are sanctified in Christ *Jesus:* So long, I say, as they truly retain this Title of the Church of Christ, as being really such, there will never be wanting the certain Judgment of Truth. For which,

The certain Judgment of Truth, is never wanting in the Church of Christ.

besides

besides the positive Promise of Christ before mentioned (which is not without Blasphemy to be called in Question, or doubted of) I shall add these Reasons. That seeing the Church of Christ is his Body, of which he is the Head, it were to make Christ negligent of his Body, who stiles himself the good Shepherd, and hath said, *He will never leave nor forsake his own*; or else (which is worse) it will infer a Possibility of *Error*, or *Mistake* in Christ, in whom as the Head, are the Eyes of the Body, by which it is to be ruled in all Things. Next, We never find in all the Scripture since the Gospel, that ever this was wanting; but that God still gave infallible Judgment by his Spirit in some of the Respects above mentioned. If the Transactions and Controversies of the after Centuries be alledged, I will boldly affirm and prove, That there was never a true Judgment wanting, so long as the Nature and *Essence* of the true Church was retained: If any will needs affirm otherwise, let them shew me where, and I shall answer it. Though I deny not (that after the Mystery of *Iniquity* did begin to work, or had so wrought, first by intermixing, and afterwards by altogether forsaking the Nature of Truth, retaining only the bare Name of the Church) but that there might be some scattered Ones, here and there one in a Nation, and now and then one in an Age, who by the Power and Virtue of the Spirit of Life working in them, might be truly sanctified; yet these were but as Witnesses in Sackcloth, no Way sufficient to give these Assemblies, in which they were engrossed, the Appellation

<small>Witnesses in Sackcloth.</small>

pellation of the Church of Christ, coming no more under Observation by the Generality, nor having, as to them, any more Influence than some little or scarcely discernable Sparks of Fire in many great Heaps and Mountains of Ashes. And thus much to prove, that where there is any Gathering or Assembly, which truly and properly may be called the Church of Christ, the *infallible Judgment* will never be wanting in Matters of Controversy.

Secondly, *That ordinarily God hath, in the communicating of his Will under his Gospel, employed such whom he had made use of in gathering of his Church, and in feeding and watching over them, though not excluding others.* For, as in a natural Body (to which the Church of Christ is compared) the more substantial and powerful Members do work most effectually; and their Help is most necessary to supply any Defect or Trouble in the Body: So also, if there be Diversities of Gifts in the Church (as is above proved) and some have a greater Measure, and some a lesser, those that have the greater are more capable to do Good, and to help the Body in its Need, than others that are weaker and less powerful. Since there are Strong and Weak, Babes and young Men, *who have overcome the evil One, and in whom the Word of God abideth*, such are more able, when the Enemy besets, to resist (having already overcome) than others who are but yet wrestling, and not Conquerors. Now, every Controversy and Dissention in the Church comes from the Besetments of the Enemy; yet if any of these strong

Assertion 2 proved.

From the Besetments of the Enemy Dissentions arise.

or young Men, or powerful Members, go from their Station, it is not denied but that they are as weak as any; and it is pre-suppoſing their Faithfulneſs in their Place that I thus affirm, and no otherwiſe. Nor yet do I limit the Lord to this Method: *For in him are all the Treaſures both of our Wiſdom and Strength*; and the weakeſt in his Hand are as ſtrong as the ſtrongeſt, who may now, as well as heretofore, kill a *Goliah* by the Hand of little *David*; yet we ſee the Lord doth ordinarily make uſe of the Strong to ſupport the Weak: And indeed, when ſuch as may be termed weak are ſo made uſe of, it alters the Nature of their Place, and conſtitutes them in a higher and more eminent Degree. For though it was little *David*; it was alſo he that was to be King of *Iſrael*. Though the Apoſtles were mean Men among the *Jews*, yet they were ſuch as were to be the Apoſtles of the Lord of Glory; Inſtruments to gather the loſt Sheep of the Houſe of *Iſrael*, and to proclaim the acceptable Day of the Lord. And though *Paul* was once accounted the *leaſt of all the Saints, a Child born out of due Time*; yet was he him who was to be the greateſt Apoſtle of the *Gentiles*.

Now then, let us conſider whom the Lord made Uſe of in the Affairs of the primitive Church, and through whom he gave forth his infallible Judgment. Did he not begin firſt by *Peter?* He was the firſt that ſpake in the firſt Meeting they had, *Acts* I. and who firſt ſtood up after the pouring forth of the Spirit; and who firſt appeared before the Council of the *Jews*, and ſpake in Behalf of the Goſpel of Chriſt: Though I am far from calling

calling him (as some do) the Prince of the Apostles; yet I may safely say, he was, one of the most *antient* and *eminent*, and to whom Christ, in a Manner somewhat more than ordinary, had recommended the Feeding of his Flock. We see also he was first made Use of in preaching to the *Gentiles*, and what Weight his and *James*'s Words had in the Contest about Circumcision towards the bringing the Matter to a Conclusion, *Acts* 15. Yet that we may see Infallibility was not inseparably annexed to him, he was found blameable in a certain Matter, *Gal.* 2. 11. notwithstanding his Sentence was positively received in many Particulars.

So also the Apostle *Paul* argues from his gathering of the Churches of *Corinth* and *Galatia*, that they ought to be Followers of him, and positively concludes in divers Things: And upon this Supposition, exhorts the Churches (both he and *Peter*) in many Passages heretofore mentioned (which I will not, to avoid Repetition, again rehearse) *to obey the Elders that watch for them; to hold such in Reputation, and to submit themselves to them that have addicted themselves to the Ministry of the Saints*, 1 Cor. 16. 15, 16.

Also, we see how the Lord makes Use of *John*, his beloved Disciple, to inform and reprove the *Seven Churches of Asia*; and no Doubt *John* (the Rest, by the usual Computation, being at that Time all removed) was then the most noted and famous Elder alive: And, indeed, I mind not where, under the Gospel, Christ hath used any other Method; but that he always, in revealing his Will, hath made Use of such as he himself had before

fore appointed Elders and Officers in his Church; though it be far from us to limit the Lord, so as to exclude any from this Privilege; nor yet, on the other Hand, will the Possibility hereof be a sufficient Warrant to allow every obscure Member to stand up and offer to rule, judge, and condemn the whole Body; nor yet is it without Cause that such an One's Message is jealoused and called in Question, unless it have very great Evidence, and be bottomed upon some very weighty and solid Cause and Foundation. And God doth so furnish those whom he raises up, in a singular Manner, of which (as I said) I mind no Instance in the *New Testament:* And in the *Old* we see, though it was strange that little *David* should oppose himself to the great *Goliah,* yet he had, before that, killed both the Lion and the Bear, which was no less improbable; and which of all is most observable, was, before that Time, by the Appointment of God, and the Hand of the Prophet, anointed King of *Israel.* Compare the 16th and 17th Chapters of the First of *Samuel.*

Assertion 3 proved. Now, as to the Third, *That any particular Persons, de* Facto, *or effectually giving out a positive Judgment, is no encroaching nor imposing upon their Brethren's Conscience,* is necessarily included in what is said before; upon which, for further Probation, there will only need this short Reflection: That for any Member or Members, in Obedience to the Lord, to give forth a positive Judgment in the Church of Christ, is their proper Place and Office, they being called to it; and so for them to exercise

exercise that Place in the Body, which the Head moves them to, is not to usurp Authority over their Fellow Members. As, on the other Hand, to submit and obey (it being the Place of some so to do) is not a renouncing a being led by the Spirit, seeing the Spirit leads them so to do: And not to obey, in case the Judgment be according to Truth, and the Spirit lead to it, is, no Doubt, both offensive and sinful. And that all this may be supposed in a Church of Christ without Absurdity, and so establish the above mentioned Propositions, will appear by a short Review of the former Passages.

If that *Peter* and *James*, their giving a positive Judgment in the Case of Difference in divers Particulars, did not infer them to be *Imposers*, so neither will any so doing now, being led to it by the same Authority: Every one may easily make the Application. And, on the Contrary, if for any to have stood up and resisted their Judgment, pretending an Unclearness, or so, and thereby held up the Difference after their Sentence, breaking the Peace and Unity of the Church (Things being concluded with an *It seemed good to the Holy Ghost, and to us*) I say, if such would have given just Cause of Offence, and have been cut off, as *Despisers of Dignities* of old, will not the like Case, now occurring, hold the same Conclusion? Now, whether those Propositions do not hold, upon the Principles before laid down and proved, I leave to every judicious and impartial Reader to judge.

Acts 15. 21.

Moreover,

Moreover, we see how positive the Apostle *Paul* is in many Particulars throughout all his Epistles, insomuch as he saith, 2 *Thess*. *ult. v.* 14. *If any Man obey not our Word by this Epistle, note that Man, and have no Company with him, that he may be ashamed.* And in many more Places, before mentioned, where he commands them both to obey him, and several others, who were appointed (no Doubt by the Spirit of God) to be Rulers among them; and yet, who will say, that either the Apostle did more than he ought, in commanding; or they less than they were obliged to, in submitting? And yet neither were to do any Thing contrary, or more than the Spirit of God in themselves led them to, or allowed them in. And if the Church of God bear any Parity or Proportion now in these Days with what it did of old (as I know no Reason why it should not) the same Things may now be supposed to take Effect that did then, and also be lawfully done upon the like Occasion, proceeding from the same Spirit, and established upon the same Basis and Foundation. And thus much, as to that Part, to shew *in whom the Power of Decision is*: Which being seriously and impartially considered, is sufficient to clear us from the Tyranny, either of *Popery* or any other of that Nature, with those that are not either wilfully blind, or very ignorant of *Popish* Principles, as the judicious Reader may observe. But seeing *to manifest that Difference* was one of those Things proposed to be considered of, I shall now come to say something of it in its proper Place.

[margin: Submission and Obedience to the Judgment of Truth, the Spirit of God leads into.]

Sec-

Section VIII.

How this Government altogether differeth from the oppressing and persecuting Principality of the Church of Rome, and other Anti-Christian Assemblies.

Whatever Way we understand the *Popish* Principles in this Matter, whether of those that are most devoted to the See of *Rome*, as the Kings of *Spain*'s Dominions, and the Princes of *Italy*; the *Jesuits*, and Generality of all those called *religious Orders*, who hold, that *Papa in Cathedra non potest errare, licet absque Concilio*; that is, *That the Pope in his Chair cannot err, though without a Council*; or of those that are less devoted, who plead this *Infallibility* in the Pope and Council, lawfully convened, who yet, by the more zealous, are reckoned *petty Schismaticks*; I say, whatever Way we take them, all those that do profess themselves Members of the *Romish* Church, and are so far such, as to understand their own Principles, do unquestionably acknowledge;

<small>Head III. Propos. 3. proved.</small>

<small>Principles of the *Romish* Church.</small>

First, *That no general Council can be lawfully called, without the* Bishop *of* Rome, *as* Christ's *Vicar, and* Peter's *Successor, call it.*   I.

Secondly, *That either he himself, or some for him, as his Legates, must be there present, and always preside.*   II.

Thirdly,

III. Thirdly, *That the Members having Vote, are made up of Bishops or Presbyters, or Commissioners, from the several Orders, being of the Clergy.*

IV. Fourthly, *That what is concluded on by* Plurality of Votes, *and agreed to by the* Pope *and his* Legates, *must necessarily be supposed to be the* Judgment of the infallible Spirit.

V. Fifthly, *That all the Members of the Church are bound implicitly to receive and believe it, because it proceeds from a Council to be accounted lawful in the Respects above mentioned, without Regard to the intrinsick or real Truths of the Things prescribed, or bringing them in any Respect to the Test or Examination of the Spirit of God in themselves, or the Scripture's Testimony, or their Agreement or Disagreement with Truths, formerly believed and received; for so much as to prove or try them by Way of Doubt, they reckon a Breach of the first Command ; as, on the other Hand, a Matter of Merit, implicitly to receive and believe them, however inconsistent with the Testimony of the Spirit in one's own Heart, Scripture, Truth and Reason.*

VI. Sixthly, *That no Man, as a Member of the Church of Christ, in that simple Capacity, unless a Clergyman, or the Ambassador of some King, &c. can be admitted to sit, vote, or give his Judgment.*

VII. Seventhly, *That it is in no Respect to be supposed, that any Members, especially* Laicks, *whether in a particular City, Country or Nation, may meet concerning any Things relating to the Faith and Worship of the Church, and give, by the Spirit*

Spirit of God, any Judgment; but that all such Meetings are to be accounted schismatical *and* unlawful. *And,*

Lastly, *That the Promise of* Infallibility, *and the* Gates of Hell not prevailing, *is necessarily annexed to the Pope and Council, called and authorized in the Manner above expressed.*   VIII.

Now, if to deny every one of these Propositions, wherein all understanding Men know the Errors and Abuses of the *Romish* Church consist, be to be *Popish*; then indeed may we be supposed to be one with the *Papists* in this Matter, but not otherwise: So that the very mentioning of these Things is sufficient to shew the Difference betwixt us and them. But if any will needs plead our Agreement with them thus;

The Papists *affirm an* Infallibility of Judgment *in the Church of Christ, and so do you; therefore you are one with* Papists.   Objection.

I answer, that proves no more our Oneness, in this Matter, than if it should be said, *The* Papists *plead that God ought to be worshipped, and so do you; therefore ye agree*: Notwithstanding of the vast differences as to that, which is not only known betwixt us and them, but betwixt them and all *Protestants*, who agree more with them in the Matter of Worship than we do.   Answer 1.

Next again, *Infallibility* in the Church (according as we hold it, and I have above defined it) no Man upon our Supposition (or *Hypothesis*) can deny it. For since we first assert, as a Principle, that no Gathering, no Church, nor Assembly of People, however true their Principles, or exact   Answer 2.

The true Church is led by the Infallible Spirit.

exact their Form be, are to be accounted the Church of Christ, except the *infallible Spirit* lead and guide; what can be the Hazard to say, that in such a Church there is still an infallible Judgment? Indeed this is so far from *Popery*, that it resolves in a Proposition quite contradictory to them. The *Romanists* say, *That the* infallible Spirit *always accompanies the outward visible Professors, and is annexed to the* eternal Succession *of Bishops and Pastors, though ever so vicious as to their Lives: Yea, though perfect* * Atheists *and Infidels in their private Judgments, yet if outwardly professing the* Catholick Faith, *and* Subjection to the Church, *they must be Partakers of the* infallible Spirit.—We say the quite Contrary: That where there is either Viciousness of Persons, or Unsoundness of Judgment in the particular Members, these cannot, by Virtue of any outward Call or Succession they have, or any Profession they make, or Authority they may pretend to, so much as claim an Interest in any Part of the Church of Christ, or the *infallible Spirit*.

* For some Popes have been known to deny, or at least to doubt the Truth of the Scriptures as to the History of Christ, and to call in Question the Immortality of the Soul, and the Resurrection.

The infallible Judgment where it is.

So then, if we admit none to be Members of the Church but such as are led and guided by the Spirit, it will be no *Popery*, in the second Place, to affirm, that where there is a Company of People so gathered, who are not any longer to retain justly the Name of the Church of Christ than they are led and guided by his Spirit,

Spirit, or a Church so qualified and designed, there is still an *infallible Judgment*. So that this *Infallibility* is not annexed to the Persons, to the Succession, to the bare visible Profession (though true, which the Church of *Rome* is denied to be) or to any Society, because of its Profession; but singly, and alone to the true, real and effectual Work of *Sanctification* and *Regeneration*, the *New Creature* brought forth in the Heart: And this is the *Spiritual Man*, which the Apostle saith, *judgeth all Things*, 1 *Cor*. 2. 15. To affirm there is an *Infallibility* here, cannot well be condemned by any; or whoso doth, must needs say, the Spirit of God is *fallible*: For we place the *Infallibility* in the *Spirit*, and in the *Power*, not in the *Persons*. And so these are the Degrees we ascend by; " Because such and such Men are led by the Spi- " rit of God, and are obedient to the Grace in " their Hearts, therefore are they Members and " Officers in the Church of Christ. And because " they are Members of the Church of Christ in " the Respect before declared, therefore there is " an *infallible Judgment* among them." We do not say, Because such Men profess the Christian Faith, and have received an outward Ordination, and so are by a lawful Succession formally esta- blished Officers in the Church, when they meet together (according to certain Rules above de- clared) there is an *Infallibility* annexed to their *Conclusions*, and they cannot but decide what is *right*; or rather, what they decide must needs be supposed to be *right*. Who seeth not here a vast Disproportion?

Now we differ herein fundamentally; that is, as to the very Basis and Foundation upon which we build; and that not only from the Church of *Rome*, but also from the Generality of *Protestants* in this Matter. All *Protestants* do acknowledge a *general Council* to be useful, yea necessary, in the Case of Division or Debate; let us consider the Basis upon which they proceed, and the Stress they lay upon it.

<small>The Constitution of a Synod, or a general Council among---</small>

<small>1 Protestants.</small>

First, All jointly, both the *prelatical* and *presbyterial*, will have this Synod or Council to consist of a Convocation of the *Clergy*, chosen and sent from the particular Congregations, with some few *laick Elders*, called together by the Civil Magistrate, in case he be one in Judgment with them.

They decide by *Plurality of Votes*. And tho' they assume not an *absolute infallibility*, in that they reckon it possible for them to err, yet do they reckon their Decisions obligatory upon their supposed Consonancy to the Scripture; and however do affirm that the Civil Magistrate hath Power to constrain all to submit and obey; or else to punish them either by Death, Banishment, Imprisonment, Confiscation of Goods, or some other corporal Pain; even though such be persuaded, and offer to make appear, that the Decisions they refuse, are contrary to the Scriptures.

<small>2 Papists.</small>

And *Lastly,* (among the *Papists*) None, tho' otherwise confessed to be a Member of the Church, both knowing and sober, except commissionate in some of the Respects

spects above declared, can be admitted to sit, vote, and give his Judgment.

Any that will be at the Pains to apply this to the Foundation I before laid of the *Infallibility* of Judgment, in that we may account only to be truly called the Church of Christ, will easily see the great Difference betwixt us, which I shall sum up in these Particulars:

> 3. We differ from them both.

First, Do we exclude any Member of the Church of Christ, that may be truly accounted so, from telling his Judgment?

> 1.

Secondly, Do we say a Man ought to be persecuted in his Outwards for his Dissent in Spirituals?

> 2.

Thirdly, Do we plead that Decision is to pass conclusive, because of the Plurality of *Votes*?

> 3.

And much more, which the Readers may observe from what is already mentioned; which, that it may be all more obvious at one *View*, will appear somewhat clearly by this following Figure; which will give the Reader an Opportunity to recollect what lay heretofore more scattered.

I. The ROMANISTS *say,*	II. The Generality of PROTESTANTS *say,*	
1. That there is an Infallibility in the Church; which Infallibility is, when the *Pope* calls a general Council of Bishops, *&c.* that whatsoever they conclude	1. That though all Synods and Councils may err; yet such Assemblies are needful for the Edification	*West. Conf. of Faith,* Chap 31.

clude and agree upon must needs be the infallible Judgment of the Spirit of God, becaufe of the Promife of Chrift, *That he would not fuffer the Gates of Hell to prevail againft his Church.*

2. And that the *Pope* and Council, made up of certain of the Clergy, having *one outward Succeffion*, and being lawfully ordained, according to the Canons, are that *Church,* to which that Promife is made, however wicked or depraved they be; yet this infallible Judgment follows them, as being neceffarily annexed to their Office, in which the Authority ftill ftands in its full Strength and Vigour.

3. So that there lies an Obligation upon the whole Body of the *Church* to obey their Decrees: And fuch as do not, are not

fication of the Church. That fuch do confift of a Convocation of the Clergy, with fome few *Laicks* particularly chofen. That all others, except thofe fo elected, have not any Right to vote or give Judgment.

2. That fuch an Affembly fo conftitute, may minifterially determine Controverfies of Faith, Cafes of Confcience, Matters of Worfhip, and authoritatively determine the fame. The Decifion is to be by Plurality of Votes, without any *neceffary* Refpect to the *inward Holinefs* or *Regeneration* of the Perfons; if fo be they be *outwardly called, ordained* and *invefted* in fuch a Place and Capacity, as gives them an Authority to be Members of fuch an Affembly.

3. What they thus decide (as they judge according to the Scripture) ought to be received with Reverence, and fubmitted

The Persecuting Church of Rome.

not only certainly *damned* for their Disobedience, but that it is the Duty of the *Civil Magistrate* to punish such by Death, Banishment or Imprisonment, &c. in case they refuse. mitted to: And those that do not, to be punished by the Civil Magistrate by Death, Banishment or Imprisonment, though they declare, and be ready to evidence, that it is because they are not agreeable to the Scripture they refuse such Decrees.

III. The QUAKERS *say*,

1. That whereas none truly ought, nor can be accounted the Church of Christ, but such as are in a Measure *sanctified*, or *sanctifying*, by the Grace of God, and led by his Spirit; nor yet any made Officers in the Church but by the Grace of God, and *inward Revelation* of his Spirit (not by *outward Ordination or Succession*) from which none is to be excluded, if so called, whether married, or a Tradesman, or a Servant. *[The sanctified Members.]*

2. If so be in such a Church there should arise any Difference, there will be an *infallible Judgment* from the Spirit of God, which may be in a General Assembly; yet not limited to it, as excluding others: And may prove the Judgment of the *Plurality*; yet not to be decided thereby, as if the *Infallibility* were placed there, excluding the fewer. In which Meeting or Assembly upon such an Account, there is no Limitation *[Their infallible Judgment.]*

tation to be of *Perſons particularly choſen*; but that all that in a true Senſe may be reckoned of the Church, as being ſober and weighty, may be preſent, and give their Judgment.

3. And that the *infallible Judgment* of Truth (which cannot be wanting in ſuch a Church) whether it be given through one or more, ought to be ſubmitted to, not becauſe ſuch Perſons give it, but becauſe the Spirit leads ſo to do; which every one coming to in themſelves, will willingly and naturally aſſent to. And if any, thro' Diſobedience or Uncleanneſs, do not all that the Church ought to do, ſhe is to deny them her ſpiritual Fellowſhip, in caſe the Nature of their Diſobedience be of that Conſequence as may deſerve ſuch a Cenſure; but by no Means, for Matter of Conſcience, to moleſt, trouble, or perſecute any in their Outwards.

—To be ſubmitted unto.

Who will be at the Pains to compare theſe three ſeriouſly together, I am hopeful will need no further Argument to prove the Difference. But if any will further object, *What if it fall out*, de Facto, *that the Teachers, Elders, or Plurality, do decide* (and from thence will ſay) *this is like the Church of* Rome, *and other falſe Churches?* It will be hard to prove that to be an *infallible* Mark of a wrong Judgment, as we have not ſaid it is of a right. And indeed to conclude it were ſo, would neceſſarily condemn the Church in the Apoſtles Days, where we ſee the Teachers and Elders, and ſo far as we can obſerve, the greater Number did agree to the *Deciſion*

Objection.

Anſwer.

cision, Acts 1. 15. For if the Thing be right, and according to Truth, it is so much the better that the Elders and greater Number do agree to it; and if wrong, their affirming it will not make it right: And truly a Gathering, where the Elders and greater Number are always, or most frequently wrong, and the younger and lesser Number right, is such, as we cannot suppose the true Church of Christ to be. And if any will plead, that there is now no *infallible Judgment* to be expected from the Spirit of God in the Church, it (no doubt) will leave the *Dissenters* as much in the Mist, and at as great a Loss, as those they dissent from; both being no better than blind Men, hitting at Random, which will turn *Christianity* into *Scepticism*. And though we may acknowledge, that this Uncertainty prevails in the Generality of those called *Churches*; yet we do firmly believe (for the Reasons above declared, and many more that might be given) That the True Church of Christ has a more solid, stable Foundation; and being never separated from Christ, her Head, walks in a more certain, steady, and unerring Path.

CONCLUSION.

A summary Recollection of the Whole. THE Substance then of what is asserted and proved in this Treatise, resolves in these following Particulars.

I. *First*, That in the Church of Christ, when it consists of a visible People (for I speak not here of the Church in the dark Night of Apostacy, that consisted not of any Society visibly united) gathered into the Belief of certain Principles, and united in the joint Performance of the Worship of God, as meeting together, praying, preaching, &c. there is, and still must be, a certain Order and Government.

II. *Secondly*, That this Government, as to the outward Form of it, consists of certain Meetings appointed principally for that End; yet not so as to exclude Acts of Worship, if the Spirit move thereunto.

III. *Thirdly*, The Object of this Government is two-fold, *outwards* and *inwards*. The *Outwards* relate mainly to the Care of the Poor, of Widows and Fatherless; where

where may be also included Marriages, and the Removing of all Scandals in Things undeniably wrong. The *Inwards* respect an Apostacy, either in Principles or Practices that have a Pretence of *Conscience*, and that either in denying some Truths already received and believed, or asserting new Doctrines that ought not to be received. Which again (to sub-divide) may either be in Things fundamental, and of great Moment; or in Things of less Weight in themselves, yet proceeding from a wrong Spirit, and which in the natural and certain Consequence of them, tend to make Schisms, Divisions, Animosities, and in Sum, to break that Bond of Love and Unity that is so needful to be upheld and established in the Church of Christ. And here come also under this Consideration all Emulations, Strifes, Backbitings, and evil Surmisings.

Fourthly, That in the true Church   IV. of Christ (according to the Definition above given of it) there will, in such Cases of Differences and Controversies, still be an *infallible Judgment* from the Spirit of God, either in one or other, few or more.

Fifthly, That this *infallible Judgment*   V. is only, and unalterably, annexed and seated in the Spirit and Power of God; not to any particular Person or Persons, Meeting or Assembly, by Virtue of any settled Ordination, Office, Place or Station, that such may have, or have had in the Church; no Man, Men, nor Meeting

Meeting standing, or being invested in any Authority in the Church of Christ, upon other Terms than so long as he or they abide in the living Sense and Unity of the Life in their own Particulars; which whosoever, one or more, inwardly departs from, *ipso Facto*, loses all Authority, Office, or certain discerning, he or they formerly have had, though retaining the true Principles and sound Form, and (may be) not fallen into any gross Practices, as may declare them generally to be thus withered and decayed.

VI.   *Sixthly*, That Jesus Christ, under the Gospel, hath ordinarily revealed his Will in such Cases through the Elders and Ministers of the Church, or a General Meeting; whose Testimony is neither to be despised or rejected, without good Cause. Neither is their taking upon them really to decide, any just Ground to charge them with Imposition, or to quarrel with their Judgment; unless it can be proved, that they are decayed, and have lost their Discerning, as above.

VII.   *Seventhly*, That to *submit* and *obey* in such Cases, is no detracting from the common Privilege of Christians, to be inwardly led by the Spirit, seeing the Spirit has led some heretofore so to do, and yet may. And that every Pretence of Unclearness is not a sufficient Excuse for Disobedience, seeing that may proceed from Obstinacy, or a Mind prepossessed with Prejudice: Yet say I not any ought to do it it before they be clear; and who are every way right, will not want Clearnefs in what they ought to do.

VIII. And, *laftly*, That thefe Principles are no ways tainted with *Impofition*, or contrary to true Liberty of Confcience: And that they fundamentally differ from the Ufurpations both of *Popery*, *Prelacy*, and *Prefbytery*, or any other of that Nature.

ROBERT BARCLAY.

F I N I S.

AN EPISTLE

TO THE

NATIONAL MEETING

OF

FRIENDS,

IN

DUBLIN,

Concerning good ORDER and DISCIPLINE in the CHURCH.

Written by *JOSEPH PIKE*.

WILMINGTON,
Re-printed by JAMES ADAMS, 1783.

AN EPISTLE

TO THE

NATIONAL MEETING, &c.

My dearly beloved Friends, and Brethren,

HAving been for some Time under a *deep* and *mournful* Sense of the States of many of the Churches of Christ, a *weighty* Concern came upon my Spirit, to communicate some of those Things to you which came under my Consideration, and I could not be easy until I had given up to do it; and as I foresee what I shall write will be *long*, and the *longer* by *commemorating* the Dealings of the LORD with us in *this* Nation, as well as by writing some Things *new* and *old :* So therefore, I desire you will bear its Length, it being, in Probability, the last Time that ever I shall write to you, for I am but *weak* in Body, and *ill* able to write at this Time; and, in all *human Prospect*, not likely to continue long in this World. But however that
may

may be, Oh! faith my Soul, that the Lord will be pleased to keep and preserve me *near* to himself to the End, that so in the End of my Time, I may attain to that everlasting Rest, that the ELDERS, who have gone before me, are already entered into.

And now, my *dear Friends*, I herewith send you the Salutation of my *endeared* Love in our LORD and SAVIOUR JESUS CHRIST, which remains as *fresh* and *fervent* with me now in *old* Age, as in my *Youth*, more especially to you that travel in *Spirit*, and are zealously concerned for the Welfare and Prosperity of SION, you are as *near* and *dear* to me as ever, and I have Unity with you, in the *Covenant* of Love and Life, whether you are *old* or *young*, *rich* or *poor*; for in this Love it is that we are bound up together in the Bundle of Life, being *baptized by one Spirit into one Body*, and in this Love which proceeds from the Spirit, the true Unity of the Church is kept up and maintained in the *Bond of Peace*, whereby the *whole Body is edified* together in Love, which you know is a *stronger* Bond and Tye than all *outward* Laws, Creeds, or Confessions of Faith *without it*.

And besides this Gift of the HOLY SPIRIT, which CHRIST has given us for our Salvation, he has given *additional* Means and Assistances *conducive* to that great End; thus he has afforded us the HOLY SCRIPTURES for our *Information*, *Edification* and *Comfort*, thro' the Spirit. He has sent us his *Ministers* and *Messengers*, whom he has furnished with the *immediate* Power of his Word: He has gifted ELDERS to *oversee*, *advise* and *admonish* us, and, by his holy Spirit, he has moved upon both Ministers and Elders, to give forth and leave

leave us *holy Instructions*, for keeping *godly* Order and Discipline in the *Churches* of CHRIST, to be as an *Hedge* and *Fence* about us for our Preservation (so far as Means can do) in this Unity of the Spirit, as well as to keep us from the *Inroads* of the Enemy, *who goes about continually seeking whom he may devour*. 1 Pet. 5. 8.

Our *gracious* LORD has done all this for us in our Day and Time, as he did formerly, so that we may truly say with that holy Prophet *Isaiah*, who spoke from the Mouth of the Lord, saying, *What could have been done more to my Vineyard that I have not done in it*. Isa. 5. 4. And I pray God it may not be said of many of us now as he said to *Israel* then, *viz. Wherefore, when I looked that it should bring forth Grapes, it brought forth wild Grapes*.

Now, my *dear Friends*, that which bears the greatest Weight upon my Spirit at this Time, is, relating to *godly* Order and Discipline in the Churches of Christ: And tho' I well know that you who have retained your *first* Love to God, and have kept your Habitation in his *holy Truth*, do not want any Information of mine to convince you of the *Necessity* and *Service* thereof; yet as *out of the Abundance of the Heart the Mouth speaketh*, so out of the abundant Concern I feel upon my Spirit for the Prosperity of Truth, I beseech you bear with me while I ease my Mind, if it but prove of the least Benefit to the Younger in your Meeting, by stirring up the *pure Mind by way of Remembrance*; for notwithstanding I am very sensible that some of you do want but little stirring up to your Duty, respecting Discipline, yet I believe many others

others do. Neither do you want to be convinced that our *Women*'s, as well as *Men*'s, Meetings for Discipline, were *first* set up by the *Movings* of the LORD's Power, through that *worthy* and *faithful* Elder GEORGE FOX; and also, that the Authority of these Meetings is to be kept up and maintained therein, you are living Witnesses thereof, because the LORD has often owned your Services in them by the *Overshadowings* of his *glorious* Power.

You know also, that in the *first Institution* of these our Men's Meetings, the Members of them were to be *faithful Men*, who were to rule and govern for the LORD, *Men fearing* GOD, *and hating Covetousness*, agreeable to those in the Apostles Times, whom the HOLY GHOST had made *Overseers* in the Church of CHRIST; yet this does not exclude *honest minded* young Men from being admitted to sit in those Meetings *as Learners*, who, growing in Truth, may at length come to have their *spiritual* Senses exercised, so as rightly to discern between *Good* and *Evil*, and *Things that differ*, tho' at first they may not see into Things *so clearly* as the *faithful* Elders did, yet as they grow in Truth, and *follow them*, as the Apostle *Paul* advises, the *Lord in due Time will reveal such Things unto them*. I can speak this from my own Experience; likewise, in a more general Way, as there are, and always will be, *different* Degrees of Growth in the Members of the Church of CHRIST, yet as all are *growing* in Truth, and drawing *one Way*, and aiming at the *same* Thing, namely the *Honour of the* LORD, and Prosperity

Exod. 18. 4.

Phil. 3 15.

of his *holy* Truth, there will be a *general* Condescension and Submission to one another, but more especially to *godly* Elders and Overseers; here the *strong* and *Self-will* of Man is kept out, and the Unity of the *Spirit*, in an *heavenly* Harmony, maintained in those Meetings, as well as among the whole Body, or Church of CHRIST.

And while Things remained in this Order, the true *Watchmen* for CHRIST, those Elders, *were good* Examples to the Flock themselves; they diligently watched them, lest the Enemy should steal in upon them; and when at any Time he made an Appearance, they gave the Alarm to the Flock to beware of the Devourer: Thus, if any Thing did appear *contrary* to Truth, of what Kind soever, then presently (without Delay) those *true Watchmen* did endeavour to put a Stop thereto; then it was that Things went well in general in the Churches of CHRIST. I could enlarge abundantly upon the good Effects of it, but stop myself, and in a few Words say, *That then the Disorderly were dealt with in due Time, according to the Nature of their Offences, and for their Good: And if they could not be reclaimed, they were set in their Places, Truth cleared, and they made as Examples to others, and then those Examples in some Measure became a Terror to such who were inclined and ready to follow their disorderly Steps, by which Means many, I believe, were deterred therefrom: And thus holy Discipline was kept in its right Channel, and, above all, the* LORD *was pleased to own those Services with his heavenly Power.*

But alas! alas! The State of Things continued in this Condition but a few Years before the Enemy
of

of all Righteousness made Attempts to break down the *Fence* of Discipline, which had been set up by the Power of GOD, and even prevailed on some who had been as *leading* Elders and Ministers to be concerned therein (such who once knew better Things) but had departed from their *first* Love to Truth, and Zeal for it; these Men, with their *libertine* Company in our bordering Nation, did rise up against that *Man* of God, *G. Fox*, who had been made the Instrument, in the Hand of the LORD, to set up good Order and Discipline; they levelled their Rage and Malice against him in particular, with those who had kept their *first* Love in general: But their *chief* End was to lay waste, and destroy this *good* Order and Discipline, and *leave every one to do as they pleased*, and would have no Bounds set, with this *plausible* Pretence, that all must be left to the Light in their Consciences, and Friends must wait until they are convinced, that such and such Things were *contrary* to Truth, tho' even many of the Things they went into, the *Light* of CHRIST led the *true* Followers of it out of, and to testify against, *in the Beginning*. This was pleasing Doctrine to *Libertines*; it took with them, and they made use of it, and thereupon went into *wrong* Liberty, as *Height, Pride, Fashions* of the *World, Stiff-neckedness, Strife, Contention*, and *so unruly*, that they would not submit their Differences to Friends, with many other Things *contrary* to Truth, too long to enumerate; and yet all this under a Pretence of *Christian Liberty*, and that they were not convinced by the *Light* in their Consciences to the contrary. In short, the Rebellion and (Confederacy against
good

good Order in the Church) was very great and strong, and in some Places they set up *separate* Meetings; but the LORD brought a *Blast* upon that Spirit, and they came to nothing, as a Body of People; yet notwithstanding this, the Seeds, which they had sown in this Time of *undue* Liberty remained, and still remain amongst many, in some Places, and in this Time it was that some of those Seeds were brought into this Nation, by Examples from them, and in particular *Height* and *Finery* in *Apparel* and *Houshold Stuff*, with some other Things, of which I am presently to speak.

Tho' I was but a *young Man* then, yet an *Eye* and *Ear* Witness of many of those Things, having been at several of the Meetings in *England*, wherein this *libertine* Spirit raised Contention, and then I clearly saw the Tendency thereof, that it would, if possible, lay waste the whole *Heritage* of GOD, and I bore my Testimony against it, as *convenient* Seasons and Opportunities offered.

I have written after this Manner to shew how *good* Order and Discipline was set up and established in a general Way, and what Spirit it was that opposed it then, and I greatly fear the same Spirit is at work now, in this Nation, tho' in a different Appearance, not by their opposing all Discipline in a general Manner as they did, but by breaking of Minutes, and weakening the Hands of the *Faithful*, who are *zealously* concerned in Spirit for the Promotion of Truth, and keeping up the Discipline thereof in its *right* Line.

Now, in opening these Things, I find I shall be still led on in an *historical* Manner, and therefore desire your Patience, and tho' it tend not to the
Infor-

Information of you *faithful* Elders in *Israel*, who know them already, yet it may be to the Younger, by *commemorating* the kind Dealings of the LORD towards us, and stirring up the *pure* Mind in them, and that none of us may be ungrateful to him, for all the Benefits and Labour that he has bestowed upon us.

I have already said that some of the Seeds, which that libertine Spirit had sown, were brought over into this Nation, and particularly that of *Height and Finery in Apparel and Houshold Furniture*, &c. And by exampling one another, they came to a great Height at last, tho' not to that Degree, as in the other Nation, but we are going fast into them.

Now, upon this Occasion, I must revive the Memory of that *Worthy* Elder, *William Edmundson*, of this Nation, whose Memory and Labours live, and are sweet to the *upright* in Heart, and who (as most of you well know) was *eminently* instrumental in the Hand of the LORD, not only in a *powerful* Ministry by Word and Doctrine, but also for establishing and maintaining *good* Order and Discipline in the Churches of CHRIST. He *zealously* and with *undaunted* Courage stood up *faithfully* for the LORD and his Cause, and opposed all *false* Liberty in its *first* Appearance, and was, to my *certain* Knowledge, much grieved, when he saw it growing in this Nation, and faithfully bore his Testimony against it, *without Favour or Affection*, and tho' he did so, and that many Epistles and Minutes went forth from our Half-year Meeting, against that *libertine* Spirit of *Height, Pride, and other Things*, that

had

had grown upon us, yet all did not prove fully effectual, until at last the LORD blest his *unwearied* Endeavours with Success, as a *chief* Instrument in the Hand of GOD, for putting *godly* Discipline in *due* and *close* Execution, by which Means a Stop was put to that Spirit, in *great* Measure, until he was taken from us, and it is now about Thirty Years since the LORD raised up and spirited many *godly* Elders to join with him as one Man, in this Work of *Reformation*, and thereupon Epistles were given forth from Half-years Meetings, which named Abundance of Superfluities, in *Apparel, House Furniture, garnishing of Houses*, &c. with *numerous* other Things relating to *Conversation* and *Behaviour*, and runing *greedily* after the Things of this World, too long to enumerate, and which may be seen in those Minutes; and for the more effectual performing this Work, they directed us to chuse out *right spirited* Friends, who had a concern upon them for the Prosperity of Truth, and putting away all those Things that were as *Nusances* in the Church, to visit every *particular* Family, to *see, inspect* and *advise* accordingly, as they saw Occasion for it.

Now, about this Time, the LORD had also raised a Concern in the Minds of the *faithful* Elders, in most Parts of this Nation, and, with them, had likewise been preparing the Hearts of a *younger* and *middle aged* Generation, to join in this Work, and when those Epistles and Minutes came down to this Province, there was a *general* Assent in the Minds of Friends to comply with the Advices they gave us, as seeing the Necessity of it;

it; and indeed I must confess, I believe that we in this City of *Cork*, were at that Time as much concerned to take the Advice as any in the Nation; for tho' our Wives and Children dressed pretty plain, yet many of them wore *rich costly* Apparel, tho' of grave Colours, and many of our Houses were furnished with *divers* Superfluities, that were not *agreeable* to the Plainness of Truth, and as Truth (I am satisfied) led into, in the Beginning.

However, so it was that the L O R D touched the Hearts of those also, and they joined *Heart and Hand* to the Work, in first cleansing their own Houses and Families from these Things, and after that, as Elders were appointed according to the Advice of the Half-year's Meeting to visit Families, so some of those, the *Younger*, were appointed amongst the Rest; but I well know it was very hard for some of them to give up to it, as thinking the Service too *weighty* for them, but having a Concern upon their Spirits, that the Work should go on, they at last complied, tho' in a Cross to their own Wills, they went in much *Weakness, Fear and Trembling*, but the L O R D (I testify) was with and strengthened them in the Service. I write this for the Encouragement of all *honest hearted young Persons*, such who are concerned in Spirit for the Prosperity of Truth, and that think themselves very weak, and thereby are *too backward* in such Services, which the *faithful* Elders in the Church of G O D shall think them measurably capable of.

It is with me to let the *Younger* know how Friends proceeded in their Visits; and this I do, in order

order to ſtir up their Minds by way of Information and Encouragement. The Viſiters choſen *firſt* met together, and, in the Love of GOD, without *Partiality*, examined one another, how far they ſtood *clear* themſelves, relating to the Things about which they were going to adviſe others; and, after due Examination proceeded thus: When we came to a Family, we ſat down with them, and firſt waited a while upon the LORD, and then, as it aroſe in the Minds of any, we principally in the firſt Place directed them to the Gift of the LORD's Spirit in themſelves, as that by which *alone* they could grow in the Truth, and which would lead them in outward Things, agreeable thereto, as to *Converſation, Behaviour and Plainneſs of Apparel and Speech,* &c. as it led our Elders in the Beginning; and that altho' theſe Things were very *commendable* in their Places, yet told them they would not do *of themſelves*, except the Heart was alſo right in the Sight of the LORD: And having ſpoken what was in our Minds, according to the State of the Family we viſited (ſometimes all together, and ſometimes particularly apart, as we ſaw Occaſion for it) we then came to the Minutes from our Half-year's Meeting, and ſpoke particularly to them.

And this I may tell you of a Truth, that in all thoſe Viſits we made in this City at that Time we met with no *Oppoſition* or *Contradiction* in any one Family or particular Perſon, that I remember; but a *general* Condeſcenſion in all, and ſometimes a *free* and *open* Confeſſion of Things that had been amiſs, and that in *great* Tenderneſs, with Hopes of Amendment for the future; ſo that the

Viſiters

Visiters and Visited had *great* Satisfaction in that Service; and this I may further tell you, above all, the LORD owned our Service, by favouring us with his holy Power therein, so that in some Families, where Things were well, the LORD overshadowed us by his *living* Presence, and melted us down together, as into one Lump; *May my Soul never forget those Times, while I have a Day to live in this World!*

Now, after those Visits were over in this City, in convenient Time most of those Visiters here did accompany some other *faithful* Elders in the Province, and they went through it, visiting the Families of Friends, like as they had done in this City, which had much the *same* Effects as here, there being *a general* Condescension to comply with the Desire of the Half-year's Meeting; and accordingly, in Time, there was (I think I may say) a pretty full and *effectual* Reformation in this Province in outward Things that had been amiss, and which that Meeting desired might be put away, and I understand the like Success attended that Service in other Parts of this Nation; and thus Things stood for several Years, and there was *great* Unity among Friends of this Province in particular, as well as in general throughout the Rest of the Kingdom, and the LORD was pleased therewith, which he manifested oftentimes by the *Overflowing* of his *divine Power* in the Meetings of Friends.

I confess, my dear Friends, my writing after this Manner looks rather like an *History* or *Narrative*, than an Epistle, but I desire you will bear with me, it being to magnify the *loving Kindness*

of

of the LORD in (rehearsing) his Dealings with us, and for the Information and Encouragement of the *Younger*, that they may follow the Steps of the *worthy Antients*, who have followed Christ, and shun and avoid that *libertine* Spirit, which I fear is now getting in, and has got in again, endeavouring to throw down and lay waste what our *godly* Elders had reared up by the *Power* of the LORD, and from this Fear I am led to query after this Manner.

Are there not some in Being who not only saw those Times of *outward* Reformation, but also heartily joined therein, by putting away out of their Houses and Families those Superfluities in *Fineness of Apparel* and *Houshould Furniture*, &c ? I am satisfied there are. Or are there any who, since that Time, have owned that Concern, and for a Time stood zealous for the Plainness of Truth ? I am persuaded there are. And now I query, are there any of late Times, of both Sorts, who have lost that former Zeal, and suffered or permitted some of the *same* or *greater Superfluities in Apparel and Dress to be worn by their Children, and in their Families ; and likewise have suffered or permitted as fine or finer House Furniture and Garnishing to come into their own Houses, or their Children's*, which I am satisfied they might have prevented, by zealously standing against it; and moreover, have they not connived at others that have gone into such Things ? I fear there are such.

Now, by these and the like Means, and by taking Examples from one another, the Seeds of *Height*, *Pride*, and *Vanity*, have grown and spread, more (among us) than ever they were before that
Time

Time of *Reformation*, to the Wounding and Grieving of the Souls of the upright in Heart. Ah! *Friends, Friends,* I have this to say to you, from the Movings of the Spirit of the LORD in my Heart, how will you answer it in the Day of Account? You, I say, that by your *Easiness* and *Lukewarmness*, have let in those offensive Things upon us again; for as our blessed Lord said, *Whoso shall offend one of these little*   Mat. 18. 6. *Ones which believe in me, it were better for him that a Millstone were hanged about his Neck, and that he were drowned in the Depth of the Sea.* What will be the Portion of such as these? Therefore let all who are concerned herein repent, and do their *first* Works, before it be *too late.*

Again, besides *Height*, *Pride* and *Fashions*, which have (I fear) appeared in too many with a *daring* Face, are there not some that have very much lost, or been ashamed of, the *plain* Language both in *speaking* and *writing.*

I further query, Are there not some who have gone into *undue* Liberty of many Kinds, and others that would be accounted *something*, who have gone into *Contentions*, *Broils* and *Differences*, (through a *covetous* and *selfish* Spirit) to the Trouble of the Church? I wish there may not. But I cannot well pass by that *evil* Spirit of Covetousness without the following Remark: "It is an
" abominable Evil in the Sight of the LORD,
" CHRIST himself severely reprehended it,
" and cautioned to beware thereof; his *holy* A-
" postles called it *Idolatry*, and the former Pro-
" phets cried out against it; as did in like
                                        " Manner

" Manner that *worthy* Elder *William Edmundſon*
" (herein before mentioned) often warning us to
" beware thereof; where it takes *deep* Root in
" the Heart, it is a *mercileſs devouring* Spirit, not
" only endeavouring to *devour* others, but even
" deſtroy that *Man himſelf* who gives Way there-
" to, and very little can ſtand before it, therefore
" beware thereof wherever it appears."

And laſtly, beſides what I have queried above, I here query in a more general Manner, Are there not ſome who were once very zealous, and ſtood againſt all thoſe Things I have mentioned, and if they had kept their Habitations in the L O R D's *holy* Truth, might have been made ſerviceable Inſtruments in his Hand, and as *bright* Stars in the *Firmament* of his Power, and have joined *Hand in Hand*, and put *Shoulder to Shoulder*, in helping the *Faithful* to keep out thoſe Things; and by which Means I am perſuaded they would in great Meaſure have been kept out: I ſay, Are there not ſome of thoſe (tho' I hope not many) that now of late Years have been *faulty* in ſome of thoſe Things themſelves, and others who have ſtood *eaſy*, and *unconcerned* in Mind, while they have ſeen and beheld ſome that were going into them, and inſtead of helping the zealous and upright in Heart, have rather *clogged* and *weakned* their Hands, by *openly* or *ſecretly* abetting the Cauſe of the wrong Spirited and the Diſorderly, ſo far as they were able, and thereby have ſometimes fended off the Stroke of Juſtice and Judgment, in the Way of Diſcipline (and hindred the Line thereof) from being ſtretched over ſuch *in due Time*, according to the Nature of their Offences: *For if right Times*
be

be not observed, right Services may be loſt. Whereas, if true Diſcipline had been duly and rightly executed, it might probably have tended to the *Good of ſuch Offenders themſelves*; as well as the *deterring others* from following their Steps; but, above all, it would have kept up, and eſtabliſhed good Order and Diſcipline in its right Line in the Church of CHRIST.

The breaking or obſtructing this right Line of Diſcipline has (I fear) produced a *partial* conniving amongſt ſome; for have not the *Eaſy, Luke-warm,* and *Indifferent* (who have loſt their firſt Love) daubed with *untempered* Mortar, while they have endeavoured to ſkreen and defend the *Covetous,* and *Troublers* of the Church? And, on the other Hand, have not ſuch joined with the *luke-warm* Daubers, when they have been juſtly found Fault withal, and then both Sorts have been eaſy with the *High, Proud* and *Libertines,* who alſo in *their turn* (as they had Opportunity) defended the Reſt; and thus they have ſtrengthened one another, contrary to that *moſt ſolemn* Charge which the Apoſtle *Paul* gave to *Timothy,* in Relation to the Management of the Church Affairs, *viz. I charge thee* (ſays he) *before* GOD, *and the* LORD JESUS CHRIST *and the elect Angels, that thou obſerve theſe Things, without preferring one before another, doing nothing by Partiality,* 1 Tim. v. 21. Such as theſe are Men for GOD, and *right* Judges for Him. They cannot ſwerve or be *partial* to any Party, Perſon, or even neareſt Relations, for *Favour, Affection,* or *worldly Ends*; but as to thoſe who are *eaſy, luke-warm, partial* or *cold,* or ſuch that are *Troublers of the Church*

Church of GOD, and who *once knew better Things*, I have this in my Heart to say (if there be any such, as I fear there are) the LORD's Controversy is against them, whether they pretend to be *Teachers* of others, or as Elders, and he will dreadfully plead with *such* above others, for they may not only have their *own* Blood to answer for, but also the Blood of others; therefore repent *in Time*, before it be *too late*. If any one shall think me *too sharp* in what I write, I may tell them it is no pleasing Work to me, for I do it in a Cross to my own Will, but the Day calls for *plain Dealing*, and I must discharge my Conscience.

But as for you, *my dear Friends*, who have retained your *first* Love to GOD, and have stood *zealous* for the LORD and his Truth, whether you are Ministers or Elders, *young or old*, what I write touches you not; therefore I verily believe you will not be offended at it, for you can discern from what Spirit I write: But notwithstanding I have enumerated so many *hurtful* Things which have prevailed upon some that have been *unwatchful*, yet I hope none will mistake me so far as that thereby I mean the Generality of Friends, which I am far from doing; for I believe, and know, that the Lord has still a *faithful* People in this Nation, which I hope he will preserve to the End.

Moreover, I have this in particular to say to you that go *mourning* under the Burden of those Things I have mentioned, be not *too* much discouraged tho' some of your Brethren, that should have helped you, have left you, it was so of old; remember that great Servant of the LORD, *Moses*, how often

he

he was brought into great Straits, by Oppositions he met with from *rebellious Israel*, yet the LORD stood by him, and carried him through to the End. Remember the *Prophets, Elijah, Ezekiel* and *Jeremiah*, with others, who sometimes thought they stood alone, yet the LORD stood by them, and likewise carried them through. Remember *Paul*, who said to *Timothy* upon Occasion, that *no Man stood with him, and all they of* Asia   2 Tim. i. 15. *turned from him*, and he oftentimes met with great Opposition and Discouragements, yet the LORD stood by him, and carried him through: These may be as Examples and Encouragements to you; therefore slack not your Hands, be not dismayed because of Oppositions and Discouragements you meet withal, stand your Ground, and be zealous for the LORD and his Testimony, and though *you cannot do all you desire, yet do all you can for him*, and the LORD will stand by you, as he did by them formerly.

  Dear Friends, there is another Thing of great Consequence that I have not yet mentioned, which has done Abundance of Mischief in the Church, and that is the *Fondness* and *Indulgence* of many *Parents* to their *Children*, in giving them their own Way and Wills so long, until the Root of Evil has grown and spread itself forth into many *evil* Branches, and at length they have been so alienated from Truth and Friends, that some of them have run quite out. I could enlarge abundantly upon the *evil* Effects of this *fond* Indulgence, but that I have been so large already on other Matters, and that we have so many Minutes against it.

However

However I say, that tho' some godly Parents have discharged their Duty to their Children, which has not had the desired Effect, yet they will be clear of their Blood; but I believe too many have not performed their Duty, by which Neglect their Children have taken wrong Liberty, and fallen into hurtful Things; such Parents must be accountable for it in the Day of the L O R D.

I have already spoken of admitting *young* Men into *Men*'s Meetings, but have this to add (not as your Director) but as believing it is what Truth will lead all *right spirited* Friends into in every Quarter, *viz.* To be very careful not to admit of any unless they come under these following Qualifications. First, They should be *sober* and *orderly* in their Conversations. Secondly, they should be *plain* and *exemplary* in their Habit, Apparel and Dressing; likewise *no Tatlers*. And thirdly, that so far as Friends can have a Sense of their Spirits, that they will be *condescending to godly* Elders, and not either in their Words or Spirits likely to oppose them, for I have observed in my Time, that some, who have been admitted, without these Qualifications, have in Time proved *great* Troublers of the Church, especially if they have had *fluent* Tongues, which I have beheld in some Places (in my former Travels) *to the Grief of my Soul.*

Another Thing I may observe to you, that we have *a great* many *young* and *middle-aged* Men amongst us, who are *orderly* in their Conversations, and also wish well to the Prosperity of Truth, and yet are (as I may term it) either *indolent,* or too much incumbered in the Things of of this World, and thereby are backward in coming up into *that Service* for Truth, which otherwife they might be capable of, were their *fpiritual* Senfes rightly exercifed, but by their being *fo backward* their Senfes grow (as it were) *dull*, for Want of Ufe, and I believe it will become the Duty of *godly* Elders in all the Meetings where fuch are, to *ftir* them up to *mind the Gift* that is in them, or if Need be, even to *roufe* them up to their Duties, as well for their own Good, as the *Service* they may have for the Truth.

And now, *dear Friends*, I am come near to an End of this very long Epiftle, and tho' I have been *thus large* already, yet *one* Thing more, bears Weight upon my Mind, and I could not be *eafy* without touching upon it, which if it fhall only tend to *a Caution* of the Younger, my End will be anfwered; and that is relating to the *clofe Joining* in Familiarity with any *dark oppofite* and *unruly* Spirits; you know we have Minutes againft it; and the Apoftle *Paul* was of the *fame* Mind, when he advifed to *have no Company with any who obeyed not their Word*, by that *Epiftle*, 2 Thef. iii. 14. 16. yet in that Cafe advifeth not *to count fuch an Enemy, but admonifh him as a Brother*, but pofitively commands, in the Name of our LORD JESUS CHRIST, to *withdraw from every Brother that walked diforderly, and not after the Tradition received of the Apoftle,* &c. 2 Thef. iii. 6. and likewife to *have no Fellowfhip with the unfruitful Works of Darknefs, but reprove them.*

Now, if any of thofe who walk *orderly*, and are

are in Fellowship with Friends, do contract a very *intimate and unnecessary Familiarity* with Persons of *dark* or *opposite* Spirits, I believe it will have these following *bad* Effects. First, it may rather strengthen them in that Spirit, than help to reclaim them from their *Opposition.* Secondly, It may harden them in *Prejudice* against those that cannot do the same. Thirdly, It may be of ill *Example*, and tend to the further Hurt of others, who are inclined to follow the Steps of the *Unfaithful.* But beyond all this, in my Time I have observed, that even the *Orderly* themselves have been *greatly* hurt, at last some of them *lost* thereby; for having these Opportunities of *frequent* Conversation together, and by the *continual* buzzing Things against the *Faithful*, the *Orderly* have in length of Time lent an Ear to them, whereby *Surmises* and *Jealousies* have been begotten, then *Hardness* and *Prejudice* have entered; and lastly, a *joining in Confederacy with dark Spirits* against those who have nothing more in their View than the *Honour* of the L O R D, and *Good of Souls*; and by this very Means (even to my own certain Knowledge) many who (at first) were *orderly* and *honest minded*, were caught in this Snare in the Time of the *Separation*, and some taken in the same in this Nation also: Therefore I hope the *Orderly* will observe our Minutes and the Advice and Commands of the Apostles, and if they have Occasion (as they may often) to converse with any of the other Sort, to *keep upon their Watch*, and carry towards them, as to

such

such who are under Admonition, for I am sure Truth will lead thereto.

And now I shall conclude in much brotherly Love, your dear Friend,

JOSEPH PIKE.

F I N I S.

www.ingramcontent.com/pod-product-compliance
Lightning Source LLC
Chambersburg PA
CBHW031748230426
43669CB00007B/530